HOW THE WORLD WORKS

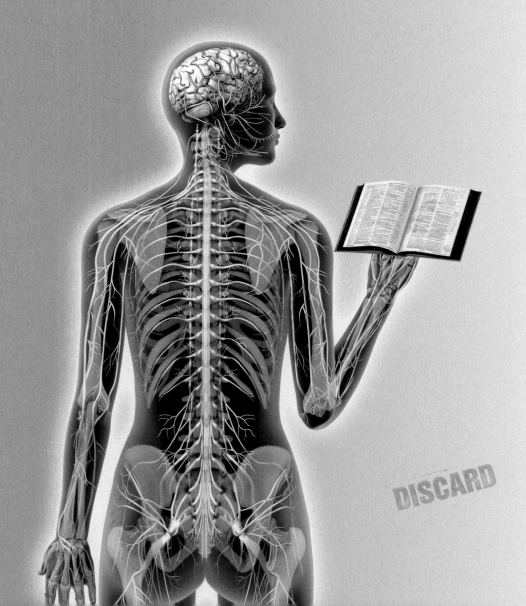

KINGFISHER
LONDON & NEW YORK

Copyright © Macmillan International Publishers 2013, 2022
First published 2013 in the United States
This edition published in 2022 by Kingfisher
120 Broadway, New York, NY 10271
Kingfisher is an imprint of Macmillan Children's Books, London

Created for Kingfisher by TallTree
2022 edition designed by Pete Clayman

Distributed in the U.S. and Canada by Macmillan,
120 Broadway, New York, NY 10271

Library of Congress Cataloging-in-Publication data has been applied for.

ISBN 978-0-7534-7818-9

Kingfisher books are available for special promotions and premiums.
For details contact:
Special Markets Department, Macmillan,
120 Broadway, New York, NY 10271.

For more information, please visit
www.kingfisherbooks.com

Printed in China
1 3 5 7 9 8 6 4 2
1TR/0122/RV/WKT/128MA

HOW THE WORLD WORKS

CLIVE GIFFORD

KINGFISHER

LONDON & NEW YORK

Earth is a very special place. Our planet is warmed by the energy of the Sun and surrounded by an atmosphere of gas. These conditions have allowed life to develop. Earth's surface is ever-changing—movements of the ground create earthquakes and volcanoes, while storms rage in the atmosphere above. Beyond Earth lie unimaginably vast regions of space containing billions of stars and galaxies.

In 1842, British scientist Richard Owen named a group of extinct reptiles dinosauria from the Greek words for "terrible" and "lizard." Since that time, millions of people have been fascinated with these creatures, which existed on Earth up until around 66 million years ago. Dinosaurs ranged in size from the size of a small bird to the length of three buses. Scientists study dinosaur remains in order to learn more about these enigmatic creatures.

65–96
LIFE

Earth is teeming with a vast range of life—from microscopic single-celled organisms to gigantic trees, blue whales, and elephants. There are believed to be more than eight million different species of living things. Scientists study the many ways they find the food and energy they need to grow and stay healthy, as well as how they defend themselves and how they reproduce.

97–128
SCIENCE AND TECHNOLOGY

Science and technology have revolutionized how we live, from powering our homes to saving lives in hospitals, and providing communications and entertainment. The results of technology range in size from microscopic electronic components to giant structures such as bridges, tunnels, and skyscrapers. Technology has even allowed us to break free from our planet to explore space.

Human history extends back many thousands of years. In that time, great civilizations have flourished, only to fade away or be conquered by invaders. Many have left behind remains—from pyramids, castles, and roads to ancient texts and mummified bodies. Archaeologists and historians study these remains to learn how people lived in the past.

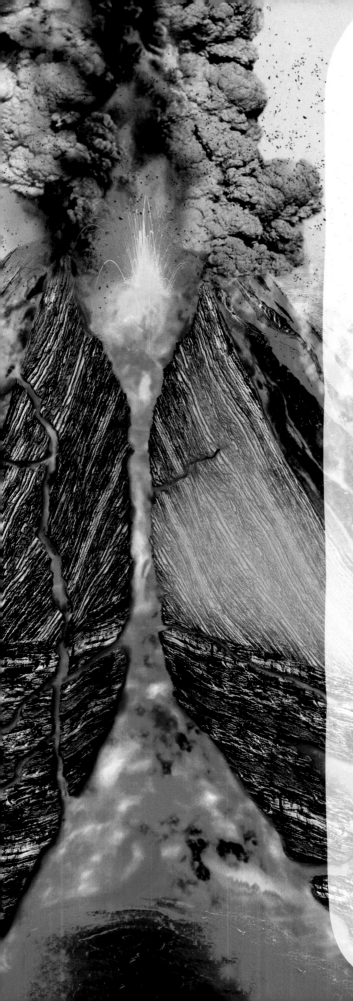

CHAPTER ONE
EARTH AND SPACE

HOW WAS EARTH FORMED?

Earth's story began about 4.6 billion years ago, shortly after the Sun started forming. Dust, ice, and rock orbiting the early Sun clumped together in larger and larger lumps that collided with one another, increasing in heat and size.

One of these, Earth, grew in size until it was large enough for its own force of gravity to attract further dust and gas. As the collisions continued, generating huge amounts of heat, early Earth's surface was repeatedly melted and reshaped. Gradually, minerals rich in iron were drawn toward Earth's center, forming a large, dense core of iron with lighter rock forming a thick layer, known as the mantle, around the iron. Over many millions of years, the planet cooled, the atmosphere developed, and rain fell, eventually forming lakes, seas, and oceans.

This image shows what Earth looked like more than one billion years ago. Basins and depressions on the surface were filled with water from rains that lasted thousands of years, creating the early seas and oceans.

Single-celled algae appeared in the sunlit areas of the oceans as early as two billion years ago.

EARTH BIRTH

Earth's formation from a glowing ball of dust and rock to the planet we know today took many hundreds of millions of years. It was almost four billion years before the first multicelled creatures appeared.

Earth begins to form as matter comes together.

Earth's surface is melted by heat from within as well as by collisions with other objects.

Intense volcanic activity generates gases, forming Earth's early atmosphere.

The planet cools, clouds form, and rain falls, producing the early seas.

Movements of parts of the crust—called plates—shape landmasses.

Meteorite impacts create craters and basins on Earth.

Huge volcanic eruptions across the planet create igneous rocks from lava flows and spew gases into the atmosphere.

Meteorite

Impact crater

MAKING THE MOON

Most astronomers believe that the Moon was formed as a result of a large body colliding with Earth some 4.5 billion years ago. Bombardment by meteorites gave the Moon its cratered surface.

Hot water rises from cracks in the ocean floor called vents.

CANADIAN SHIELD

Snug Harbor on Lake Huron is part of a rocky geological feature known as the Canadian Shield. It features some of the oldest rocks found on Earth, dated to at least 3.8 billion years ago.

Igneous rocks lie on ancient volcanic bedrock.

HOW DO THE CONTINENTS MOVE?

Earth's surface is made of a rocky crust. This crust is not one single piece, but is broken up into a number of giant slabs known as plates, some of which form the world's continents. These sit on top of the mantle—the layer below the surface.|

The mantle is about 1,800 mi. (2,900km) thick and ranges in temperature from about 1,830 to 5,970°F (1,000 to 3,300°C). Heat currents inside the mantle cause the plates above to move by a small amount—between 0.8 and 4 in. (2 and 10cm) each year. This may not sound like a lot, but over millions of years it means that the continents travel significant distances. Plates can move apart from one another or crash together. When they crash, a plate can deform, grind past, or slide under another plate. These movements generate earthquakes and volcanic eruptions, and create mountain ranges.

DRIFTING APART

About 250 million years ago (mya), all land was part of one supercontinent that scientists call Pangaea. Over time, this supercontinent broke up into smaller continents that began to drift.

1. 225 mya—Pangaea is one supercontinent.

2. 200 mya—Pangaea splits into two sections.

3. 135 mya—the Americas start to move away from Africa and Europe as the Atlantic Ocean widens.

4. Today—Africa is moving north while Asia and North America are moving toward each other.

The continental crust varies in thickness from about 15.5 to 43.5 mi. (25 to 70km).

Africa lies on the African plate, which for about 100 million years has been moving in a northeasterly direction toward the Eurasian plate. Scientists estimate that it is moving at a rate of about 1 in. (2.5cm) per year.

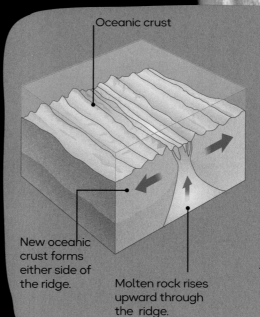

Oceanic crust

New oceanic crust forms either side of the ridge.

Molten rock rises upward through the ridge.

SPREADING CRUST

In the middle of Earth's oceans, new crust forms and spreads between plates. Molten rock rises up through cracks where it cools and hardens in the cold water, creating new oceanic crust. Long chains of undersea mountains lie along these mid-oceanic ridges.

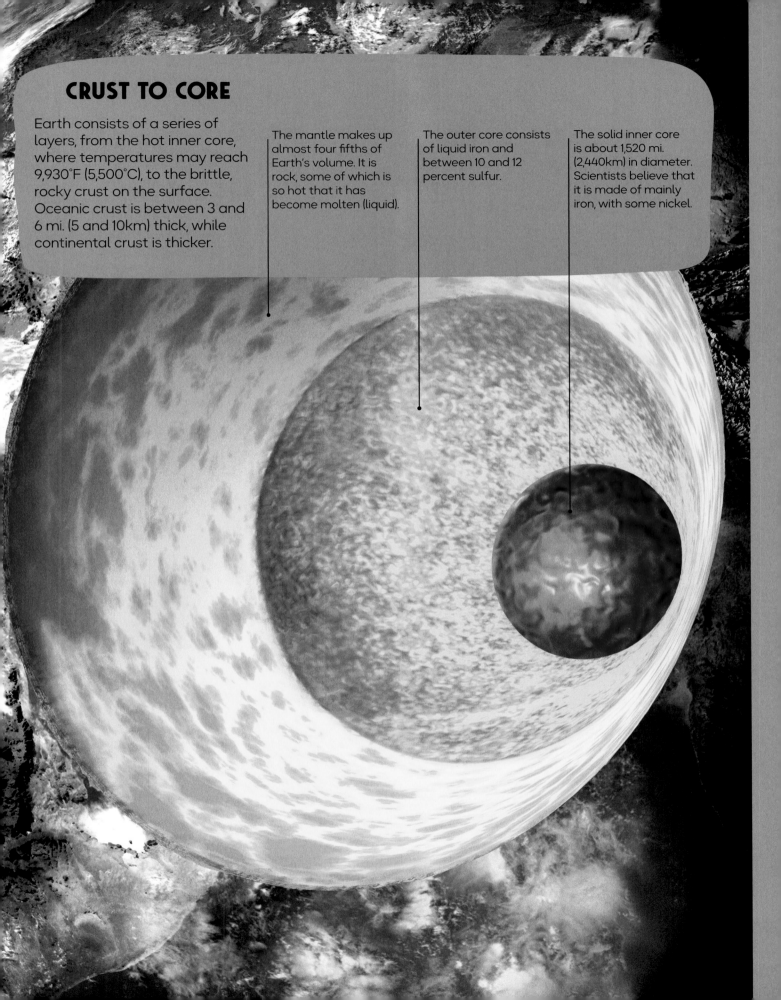

CRUST TO CORE

Earth consists of a series of layers, from the hot inner core, where temperatures may reach 9,930°F (5,500°C), to the brittle, rocky crust on the surface. Oceanic crust is between 3 and 6 mi. (5 and 10km) thick, while continental crust is thicker.

The mantle makes up almost four fifths of Earth's volume. It is rock, some of which is so hot that it has become molten (liquid).

The outer core consists of liquid iron and between 10 and 12 percent sulfur.

The solid inner core is about 1,520 mi. (2,440km) in diameter. Scientists believe that it is made of mainly iron, with some nickel.

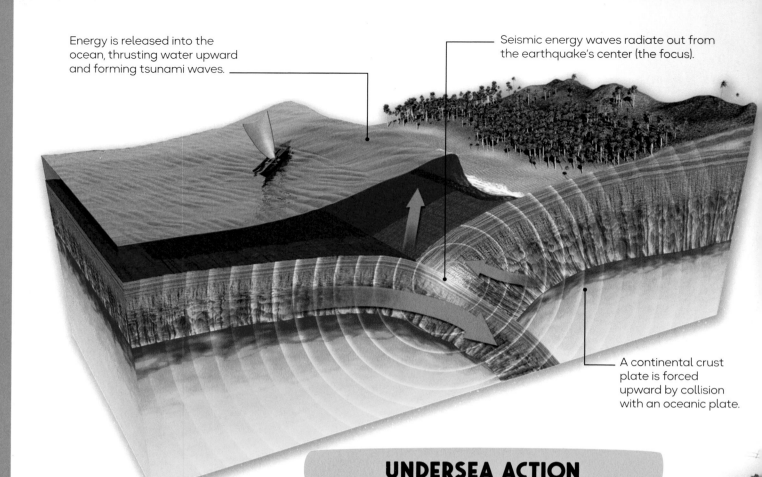

Energy is released into the ocean, thrusting water upward and forming tsunami waves.

Seismic energy waves radiate out from the earthquake's center (the focus).

A continental crust plate is forced upward by collision with an oceanic plate.

UNDERSEA ACTION

An undersea earthquake often occurs when two plates collide and one plate subducts (slides down) below the other plate. As the energy generated by the quake reaches the seabed, water is thrust upward, forming a tsunami.

HOW DO EARTHQUAKES CAUSE TSUNAMIS?

A tsunami is a series of giant waves that can travel quickly across an ocean and strike land with devastating force. Some tsunamis are caused by undersea volcanoes erupting or by an enormous underwater landslide but most are the result of earthquakes.

An earthquake is a sudden release of built-up energy from Earth's crust. Most earthquakes are caused by the extreme forces and pressures that exist near faults—where two plates grind against each other or collide. As the rocks suddenly release this pressure in the form of energy waves, any water above the earthquake can be jolted upward with great force, creating powerful waves. Out in the ocean, tsunami waves travel very fast, at speeds of up to 600 mph (960km/h). However, as they approach the coast, they slow down to 62 mph (100km/h) as the waves grow in height, forming a wall of water that crashes over the land.

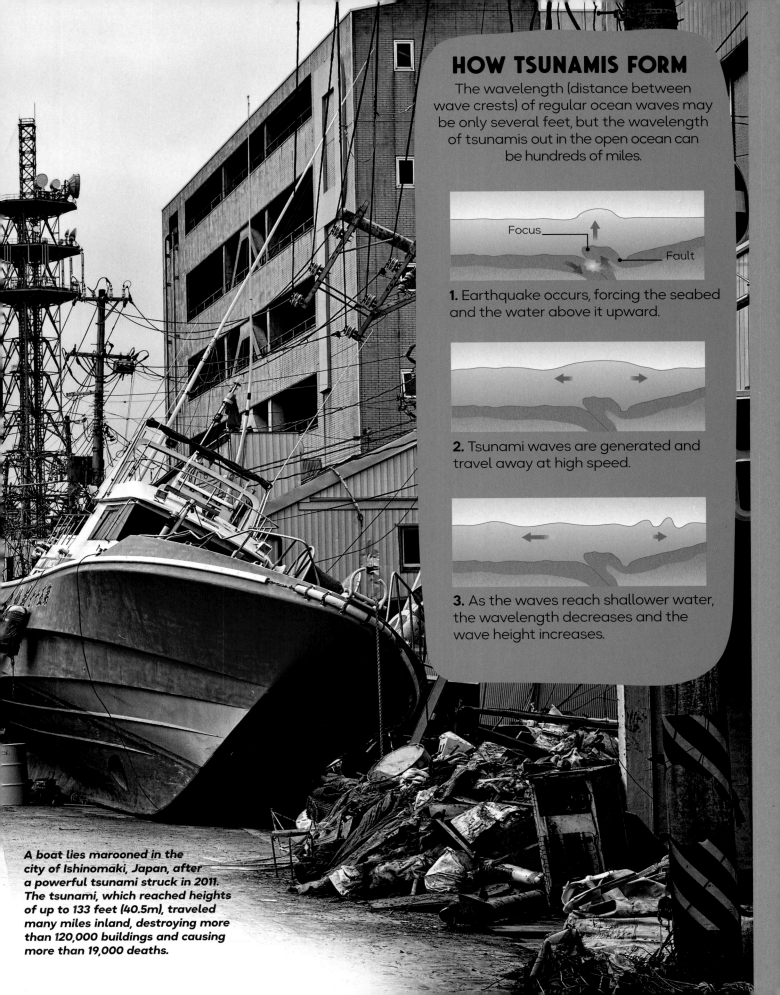

HOW TSUNAMIS FORM

The wavelength (distance between wave crests) of regular ocean waves may be only several feet, but the wavelength of tsunamis out in the open ocean can be hundreds of miles.

Focus — Fault

1. Earthquake occurs, forcing the seabed and the water above it upward.

2. Tsunami waves are generated and travel away at high speed.

3. As the waves reach shallower water, the wavelength decreases and the wave height increases.

A boat lies marooned in the city of Ishinomaki, Japan, after a powerful tsunami struck in 2011. The tsunami, which reached heights of up to 133 feet (40.5m), traveled many miles inland, destroying more than 120,000 buildings and causing more than 19,000 deaths.

HOW DO VOLCANOES ERUPT?

Volcanoes are openings in Earth's crust through which molten rock—called magma—along with ash and gases, reach the surface. This process can be a gentle oozing or an explosive, destructive eruption.

Magma is rock deep underground that is heated so much that it flows. Less dense than the surrounding rock, magma may rise and gather in underground pockets known as magma chambers. Sometimes, pressure builds up and forces the magma upward through cracks in Earth's crust. Magma that reaches the surface is known as lava and ranges in temperature from 1,300 to 2,200°F (700 to 1,200°C). The hotter the lava, the thinner and runnier it is. Thick, sticky lava containing a lot of trapped gas can cause violent eruptions. One such eruption happened in 1980 in the United States, when the top 1,300 ft. (400m) of Mount St. Helens was blown away.

This volcano is erupting violently, spewing many tons of ash and gas high up into the air while red-hot lava runs down its slopes, destroying everything in its path.

Magma may also reach the surface through secondary side vents in the volcano's structure.

Thick, slow-flowing lava travels shorter distances and helps form this steep-sided cone volcano.

LAVA FLOWS

Here, lava flows into the sea. When lava cools, it hardens to form one of a number of types of igneous rock such as basalt, obsidian, or rhyolite.

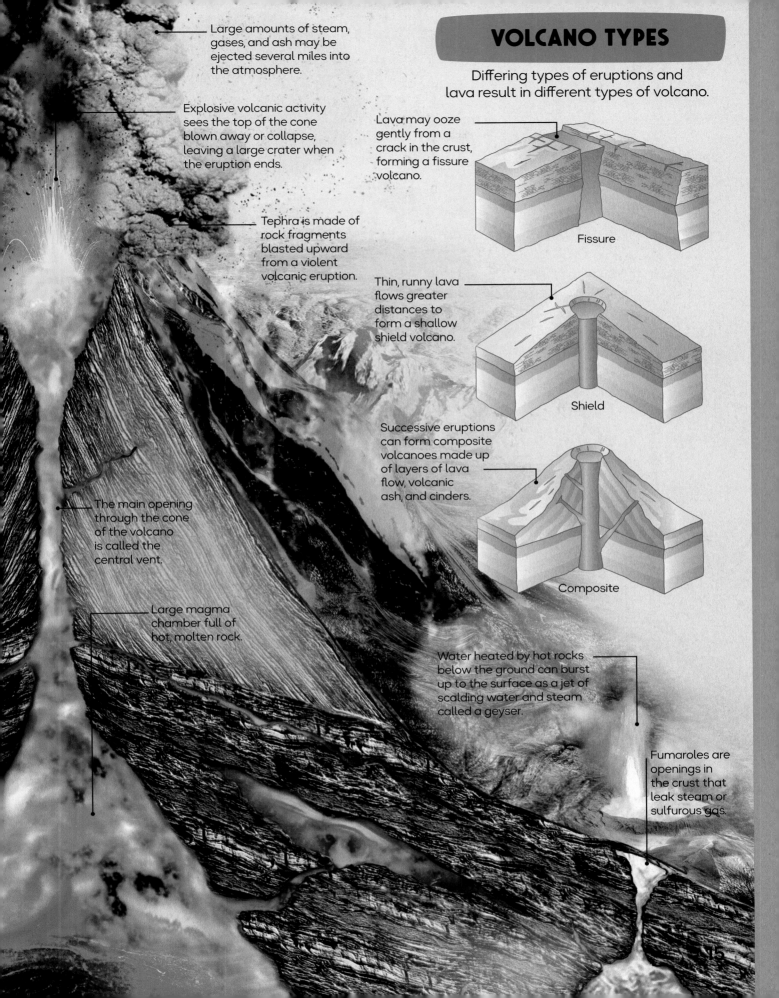

Large amounts of steam, gases, and ash may be ejected several miles into the atmosphere.

Explosive volcanic activity sees the top of the cone blown away or collapse, leaving a large crater when the eruption ends.

Tephra is made of rock fragments blasted upward from a violent volcanic eruption.

The main opening through the cone of the volcano is called the central vent.

Large magma chamber full of hot, molten rock.

VOLCANO TYPES

Differing types of eruptions and lava result in different types of volcano.

Lava may ooze gently from a crack in the crust, forming a fissure volcano.

Fissure

Thin, runny lava flows greater distances to form a shallow shield volcano.

Shield

Successive eruptions can form composite volcanoes made up of layers of lava flow, volcanic ash, and cinders.

Composite

Water heated by hot rocks below the ground can burst up to the surface as a jet of scalding water and steam called a geyser.

Fumaroles are openings in the crust that leak steam or sulfurous gas.

15

HOW DO MOUNTAINS RISE AND FALL?

Mountains are landmasses raised steeply above the surrounding land. They are formed in a number of different ways, but mostly through the interaction of the plates in Earth's crust. Eventually, mountains are worn away by erosion.

Earth's crust is mainly made of hard rock, but immense pressure—brought about by movement of the plates—causes the rock to buckle and bend, or fold over on itself in layers. These layers eventually build up to form large mountain ranges. Examples of these are the Rockies in North America, the Himalayas in Asia, and the Andes in South America. Other mountains rise where cracks in Earth's crust allow giant blocks of land to be forced upward. The Himalayas and other young mountains are still on the rise, but many mountains are decreasing in height as they are worn down by water, wind, icy glaciers, and other types of erosion.

This landscape shows the many factors that lead to the formation of mountains—from the slow movement of giant blocks of crust, up and down, to sudden volcanic activity.

Block mountains have a flat top with steep cliffs on either side.

This fault is a significant crack in Earth's crust.

A block mountain forms where a block of crust is forced upward by plate movements.

Pressure beneath the surface cracks the crust into blocks. This block has sunk down to form a rift valley.

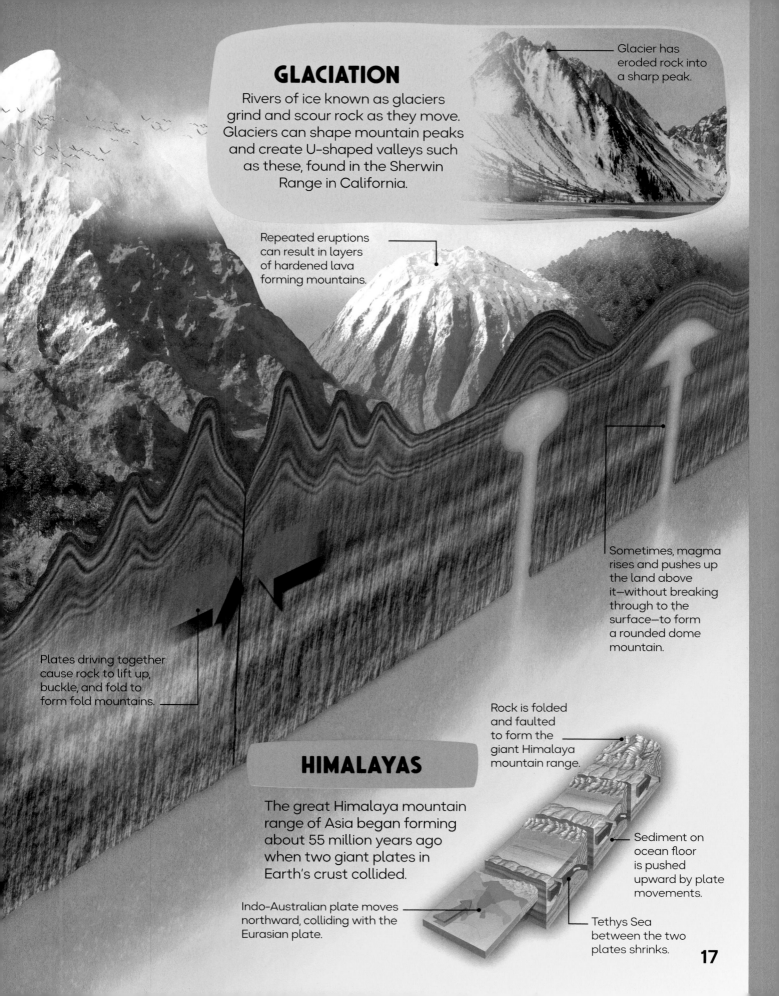

GLACIATION

Rivers of ice known as glaciers grind and scour rock as they move. Glaciers can shape mountain peaks and create U-shaped valleys such as these, found in the Sherwin Range in California.

Glacier has eroded rock into a sharp peak.

Repeated eruptions can result in layers of hardened lava forming mountains.

Sometimes, magma rises and pushes up the land above it—without breaking through to the surface—to form a rounded dome mountain.

Plates driving together cause rock to lift up, buckle, and fold to form fold mountains.

Rock is folded and faulted to form the giant Himalaya mountain range.

HIMALAYAS

The great Himalaya mountain range of Asia began forming about 55 million years ago when two giant plates in Earth's crust collided.

Sediment on ocean floor is pushed upward by plate movements.

Indo-Australian plate moves northward, colliding with the Eurasian plate.

Tethys Sea between the two plates shrinks.

17

HOW DO CLOUDS FORM?

Clouds form through evaporation and condensation. When water is heated, it evaporates and turns into a gas called water vapor. The warm air containing the water vapor is lighter than the liquid water, so it rises. In the sky, the water vapor condenses into a cloud.

As the warm air containing water vapor rises and cools, condensation changes the vapor into millions of small water droplets. This process can be caused by the Sun heating the planet's surface, forcing air to rise over hills and mountains, or when a mass of warm air rises up over a mass of heavier, colder air. As the water droplets collide with each other, they form larger, heavier drops and visible clouds. When the droplets become too heavy for the air to support, they fall as precipitation—rain, snow, hail, or sleet (a mixture of rain and snow).

Clouds are a vital part of the water cycle. Driven by the Sun's energy, the cycle is the never-ending sequence of water circulating between Earth's surface and its atmosphere.

The Sun's heat energy helps water evaporate from oceans, lakes, and rivers into the atmosphere.

Water returns to the planet's surface, falling as rain, snow, or hail.

Fluffy cumulus clouds mostly form when warm air rises and reaches a level of cooler air.

CLOUD TYPES

Cirrus

Cirrocumulus

Cirrostratus

Altocumulus

Cumulonimbus

Stratus

Plants also release water into the atmosphere via the process of transpiration.

Different types of clouds form at different altitudes. These range from ground-hugging stratus clouds to cirrus clouds that form 20,000 ft. (6,000m) or more above the ground.

In very cold air, water droplets freeze into ice crystals, which form snowflakes.

Clouds can travel long distances, moved by winds and air currents.

Snowfall on mountains melts in the summer to feed streams and lakes.

Water seeps through cracks in the ground to form a layer of groundwater. The surface of this water is called the water table.

Water runs in streams and rivers from higher altitudes down toward sea level.

STORM FORMING

Storm clouds form when rapidly rising warm, moist air reaches cooler parts of the atmosphere.

1. Warm, moist air rises and cools to form cumulus clouds.

2. Rain, snow, or hail falls from cumulonimbus clouds, dragging cold air down.

3. An increase of cold air flowing downward breaks up storm clouds.

A number of thunderstorms form as clouds.

A large hurricane forms from a series of thunderstorms generated above a tropical region of the Atlantic Ocean, where the hurricane season lasts from June to November.

The storm grows in size and, as it spins, becomes circular in shape.

HOW DOES A HURRICANE BEGIN?

Hurricanes—or to give them their scientific name, tropical cyclones—are giant, spiraling storms with ferocious wind speeds. They form out in the oceans and can wreak havoc and destruction if they travel over land.

Hurricanes form over the tropical ocean waters near the equator, where the Sun evaporates the warm waters quickly, creating moisture in the air that can form a series of thunderstorms. These storms merge together, growing as more heated air moves upward. When hit by winds, they start to spin and a hurricane is formed. As more hot air is sucked into the storm, and as cold air is drawn into its center from above, the hurricane can reach between 62 and 1,242 mi. (100 and 2,000km) in diameter. Its winds swirl around at speeds as high as 200 mph (320km/h).

TROPICAL CYCLONE CONDITIONS

A hurricane needs ocean water with temperatures higher than 80°F (27°C) to provide the energy and rapid evaporation that forms its heavy storm clouds.

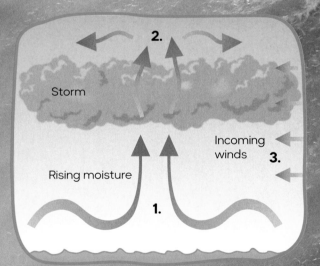

Storm

Incoming winds

Rising moisture

2.

3.

1.

1. Warm air carrying a lot of moisture rises to form the storm's clouds.

2. Winds force air upward. This lowers air pressure, which draws more air upward into the storm.

3. Winds outside the hurricane may move it hundreds of miles during the week or so that it lasts.

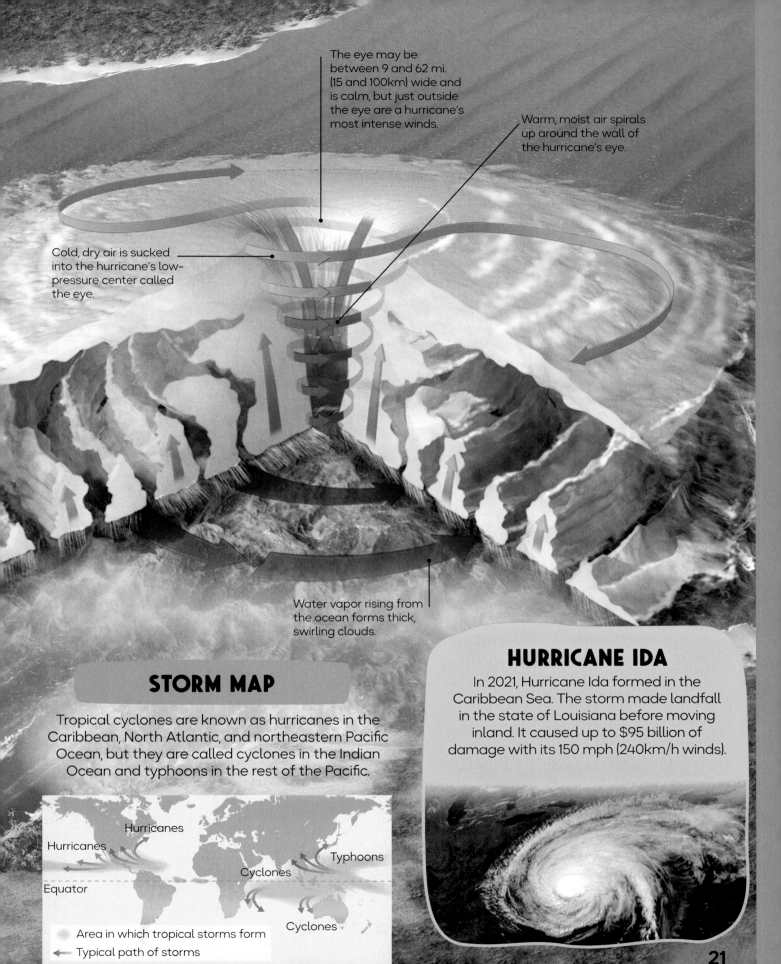

The eye may be between 9 and 62 mi. (15 and 100km) wide and is calm, but just outside the eye are a hurricane's most intense winds.

Warm, moist air spirals up around the wall of the hurricane's eye.

Cold, dry air is sucked into the hurricane's low-pressure center called the eye.

Water vapor rising from the ocean forms thick, swirling clouds.

STORM MAP

Tropical cyclones are known as hurricanes in the Caribbean, North Atlantic, and northeastern Pacific Ocean, but they are called cyclones in the Indian Ocean and typhoons in the rest of the Pacific.

Hurricanes
Hurricanes
Typhoons
Cyclones
Equator
Cyclones

Area in which tropical storms form
Typical path of storms

HURRICANE IDA

In 2021, Hurricane Ida formed in the Caribbean Sea. The storm made landfall in the state of Louisiana before moving inland. It caused up to $95 billion of damage with its 150 mph (240km/h winds).

HOW DO CORAL REEFS FORM?

Coral reefs may occupy less than one percent of the world's oceans, but they provide incredibly rich habitats for life. These structures are often large, and they are actually formed by tiny marine creatures called coral polyps.

Corals are fixed in one place but use their tentacles to catch prey, which ranges from microscopic plankton to small fish. Scientists have identified more than 1,300 different types of coral. Corals are divided into two groups: soft corals that have a leathery outer surface, and stony corals that create reefs. Stony corals secrete calcium carbonate, or limestone, from their base. These substances form a hard skeleton that offers the corals protection from predators. The skeleton remains after the coral dies. Over time, as coral reproduces and spreads, the skeletons mount up and join other colonies, and the coral reef grows.

The Great Barrier Reef off the northeastern coast of Australia is the largest coral reef system in the world. Made up of as many as 400 different corals, its collection of more than 2,500 individual reefs provides a habitat for some 1,500 species of fish.

CORAL FEED

A coral catches some prey by stinging it with its tentacles. However, most of a coral's nutrients come from tiny algae living within the coral's tissue. Coral and algae alike require plenty of sunlight.

A small, neon goby is prey for the coral.

Tiny tentacles cover the surface of a brain coral.

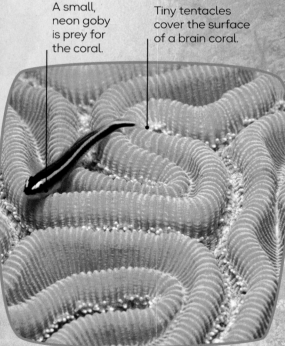

Many species of octopus make their home among coral reefs.

Many corals are brightly colored underwater but lose their color when they die or are taken out of the water.

The base of the coral is attached to rock on the seabed.

Some corals have an intricate branching structure like a tree.

REEF TYPES AND ATOLLS

An atoll is formed when a reef continues to grow upward from a volcanic island that has submerged below sea level. Most atolls are in the Pacific Ocean.

1. Fringing reefs are corals that grow from an island shore into the sea.

Shoreline

Barrier reef

2. Barrier reefs form as a volcano sinks. It is separated by a lagoon of open water between the reef and the shore.

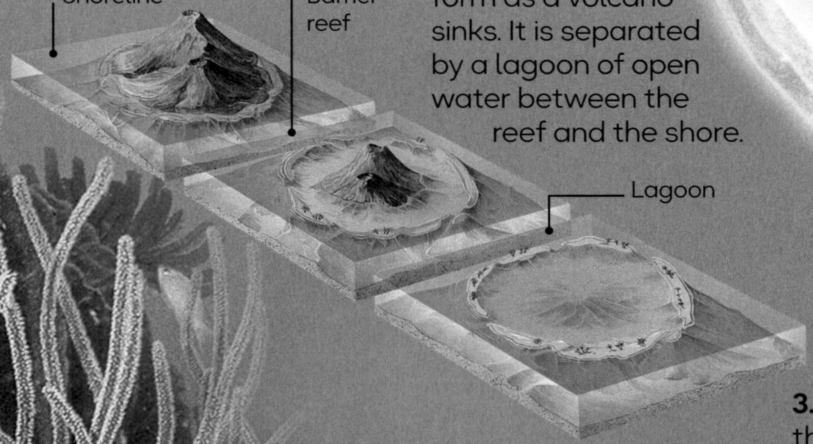

Lagoon

Coral reefs provide homes for 25 percent of all the world's marine species, including worms, mollusks, crustaceans (such as crabs), and jellyfish.

Delicate corals are at risk from physical impact by humans and larger marine creatures, as well as pollution.

3. An atoll is a reef that forms a circular shape, inside which may be a calm lagoon.

DYING CORAL REEFS

Coral reefs around the world are under threat due to warming oceans, pollution, and overfishing. Scientists are looking for ways to protect corals. One option is to create "national parks" in the oceans, which would be marine protected areas.

HOW ARE DESERTS CREATED?

Deserts are dry regions of land where little water falls from the atmosphere to the ground—usually less than 10 in. (25cm) in total each year. This lack of rain or snowfall occurs for varying reasons in different parts of the world.

Many of the world's deserts, including the Sahara and the Kalahari, are found in subtropical regions where belts of warm, dry, sinking air carry little rainfall. Some deserts are formed because of rain shadows (see right), while continental deserts arise in regions a long way inland and away from the moist air and rainfall of coastal areas. Deserts can also spread because of climate change or human activity. In hot, dry regions near deserts, overgrazing by livestock can clear land of its plant cover. With the loose soil blown or washed away, moisture is not kept in the land and desert conditions can occur.

Desert eagles seek out rodents and other desert creatures to hunt.

A hot desert often experiences baking-hot temperatures during the day, but with few clouds or plants to hold in heat, freezing cold temperatures at night. Deserts pose great survival challenges to the plants and creatures that live in them.

Winds carrying sand act as a powerful abrasive, wearing away softer rock to form these unusual pillars.

A cactus stores water in its fleshy stem.

Desert mammals, such as this sand cat, need to shade themselves from the hot sun.

DIFFERENT DESERTS

Deserts occupy about one third of the planet's land surface, but only about one fifth of desert lands are covered in sand. Other deserts have different types of surfaces.

Snow, ice, and, where exposed, bare rock and gravel.

Cold desert

Surface covered in thick sand, often blown into dunes.

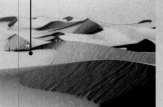

Sandy desert

Bare rocky plains strewn with stones.

Stony desert

Sand is blown by winds into distinctive sloped mounds called dunes.

Sidewinder snakes, found in North American deserts, slide sideways to glide across the loose sand.

Fennec foxes live in the Sahara. During the day, they hide away burrows, and are active during the night when it is cooler.

RAIN SHADOW DESERTS

As full clouds travel over mountains, they cool and release their moisture as rain. The dry air travels over the mountains to the land on the far side, creating a rain shadow desert.

Rising air cools

Dry air, carrying little moisture, travels over the mountain

Prevailing (usual) wind direction

Warm, moist air rises

Water vapor condenses and falls as rain

Rain shadow

The desert cottontail is a rabbit found in the southwestern United States. It requires little water, surviving on the moisture in the plants it eats.

HOW DOES THE SUN SHINE?

The Sun is the giant, glowing star at the heart of the solar system. This glowing ball of gas is so massive that it makes up more than 99.5 percent of all matter found in the solar system.

The core of the Sun is a giant nuclear furnace fueled every second by hundreds of millions of tons of hydrogen gas. Nuclear power stations on Earth split atoms to generate large amounts of energy, but the Sun works in a different way. It fuses (joins) the nucleus of hydrogen atoms together to create helium atoms. The vast amounts of energy this generates travel up through the Sun's radiative and convective zones to the surface, which is known as the photosphere. Energy is radiated out through the solar system by the Sun in the form of light and heat. Light waves from the shining Sun take about eight minutes to reach Earth.

The Sun consists of about 74 percent hydrogen, 25 percent helium, and small amounts of other elements. Energy is generated in its core and travels through its different layers or zones before being radiated out into the solar system.

The Sun is so large that more than 1.3 million planet Earths would fit inside it.

NUCLEAR FUSION

Temperatures of about 27 million°F (15 million°C) and vast pressures inside the Sun's core force the nuclei of different types of hydrogen atoms (deuterium and tritium) to fuse together, creating the nuclei of helium atoms—plus energy.

Tritium atom nucleus contains one proton and two neutrons.

Deuterium atom nucleus contains one proton and one neutron.

Fusion generates a large amount of energy.

A spare neutron from the reaction may react with other atoms.

Fusion reaction joins atoms together to form the nucleus of a helium atom.

Sunspots are cooler areas of the Sun's surface, which appear darker.

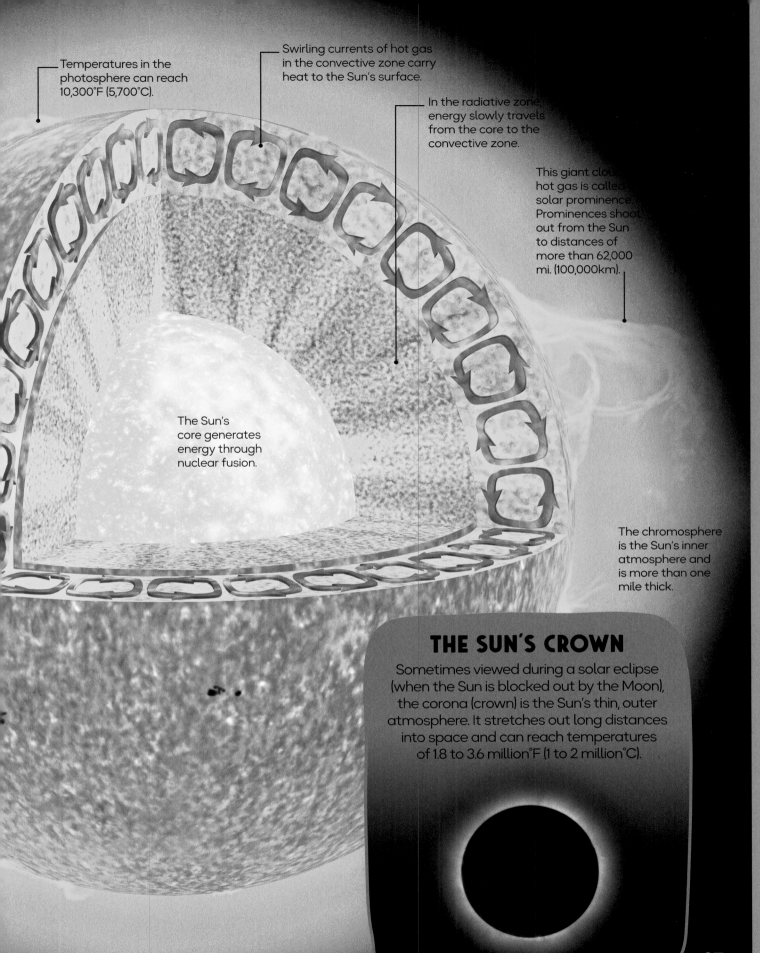

Temperatures in the photosphere can reach 10,300°F (5,700°C).

Swirling currents of hot gas in the convective zone carry heat to the Sun's surface.

In the radiative zone, energy slowly travels from the core to the convective zone.

This giant cloud of hot gas is called a solar prominence. Prominences shoot out from the Sun to distances of more than 62,000 mi. (100,000km).

The Sun's core generates energy through nuclear fusion.

The chromosphere is the Sun's inner atmosphere and is more than one mile thick.

THE SUN'S CROWN

Sometimes viewed during a solar eclipse (when the Sun is blocked out by the Moon), the corona (crown) is the Sun's thin, outer atmosphere. It stretches out long distances into space and can reach temperatures of 1.8 to 3.6 million°F (1 to 2 million°C).

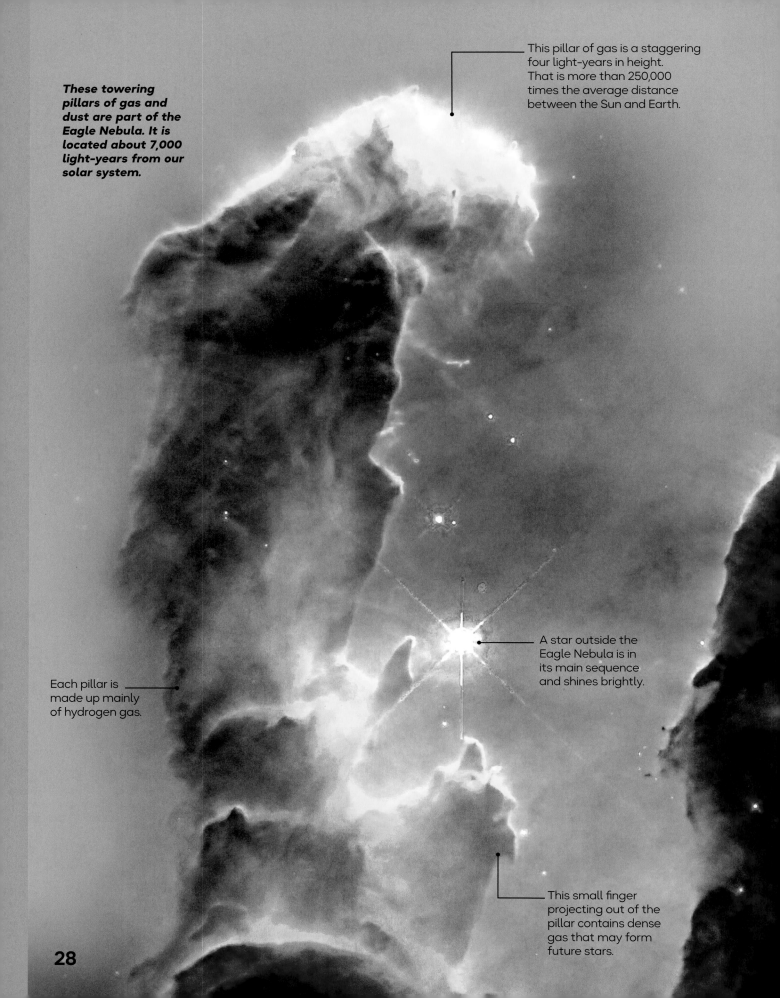

These towering pillars of gas and dust are part of the Eagle Nebula. It is located about 7,000 light-years from our solar system.

This pillar of gas is a staggering four light-years in height. That is more than 250,000 times the average distance between the Sun and Earth.

Each pillar is made up mainly of hydrogen gas.

A star outside the Eagle Nebula is in its main sequence and shines brightly.

This small finger projecting out of the pillar contains dense gas that may form future stars.

STAR BIRTH

Dust and gas is unevenly spread throughout a stellar nursery. This unevenness causes clumps to form, and these eventually become shining stars.

1. Gas and dust are pulled inward by the force of gravity and clump together.

2. The clumps collapse in on themselves, getting hotter and denser.

3. Pressure and density of the core grow until nuclear fusion begins.

4. Nuclear fusion generates vast amounts of energy, which blasts away surrounding gas and dust.

HOW IS A STAR CREATED?

Stars are giant balls of gas that burn fiercely. Most are born in great stellar "nurseries" known as nebulae. These vast regions in space are made up of giant clouds of gas and large amounts of dust.

The force of gravity, sometimes caused by an explosion or collision, often triggers star formation. Inside a nebula cloud, gravity makes gas and dust pull together into a clump, which increases in density and temperature. Pressure and heat build at the center, known as the core, and this generates more gravity and pulls in more and more gas and dust until a protostar—a new star in the making—is formed. If the protostar is large enough, and dense and hot enough, nuclear fusion reactions begin (see pages 26–27) and the star begins to emit huge amounts of energy.

Young stars shine through the gaseous clouds.

ORION NEBULA

The star nursery nearest to Earth is the Orion Nebula, about 1,400 light-years away. It is huge, measuring up to 50 light-years across, and is home to thousands of young stars and protostars. On a clear night, it is visible to the naked eye in the constellation Orion.

This black hole formed when a massive star core collapsed in on itself following a supernova explosion. The black hole is so dense and its gravity so strong that everything close by is pulled into it.

DIFFERENT ENDINGS

Stars die in different ways depending on their mass—the amount of matter they contain. Here are three common endings for stars.

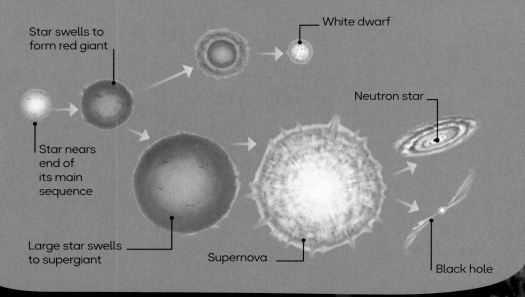

Star swells to form red giant

White dwarf

Star nears end of its main sequence

Neutron star

Large star swells to supergiant

Supernova

Black hole

HOW DO STARS DIE?

Stars begin to die when they run out of the hydrogen that fuels the nuclear reactions in their core. The smallest stars, smaller than the Sun, cool and shrink to form what are known as white dwarfs, which slowly fade. Larger stars end more dramatically.

When an average-size star, like our Sun, nears the end of its life, it swells in size and casts off many of its outer layers. The shrinking, cooling remains of the star become a white dwarf, which gradually dwindles in energy over millions of years. Massive stars, far bigger than the Sun, die more spectacularly. After swelling to a supergiant, a massive star's core collapses, creating temperatures as high as 18,000 million°F (10,000 million°C) before a supernova explosion blows away the star's outer layers with great force. Sometimes, this leaves behind a small, very dense body called a neutron star.

A jet of matter is ejected from the center of some black holes, a phenomenon not yet understood by scientists.

Nothing can escape the intense pull of a black hole, not even light.

Disk of spinning matter being drawn into the black hole.

SWELLING UP

The Sun will not run out of fuel and die for many billions of years, but when it does, it will first swell in size to become a red giant. It will become so large that its outer reaches will engulf the planets in our solar system closest to it, including Earth.

EARTH AND SPACE
FIND OUT MORE ABOUT HOW THE WORLD WORKS

WEBSITES TO VISIT

https://kids.britannica.com/kids/article/plate-tectonics/346101
See inside our planet and learn about the movement of plates of crust with this informative website.

www.natgeokids.com/uk/discover/geography/physical-geography/tsunamis/
Read up on how tsunamis and learn about how they're caused, how big they can be, and what happens in the aftermath.

www.geology.sdsu.edu/how_volcanoes_work
View images of famous eruptions and read about the different types of volcanoes found on Earth.

https://gpm.nasa.gov/education/videos/water-cycle-animation
Watch this clear animation of the water cycle in action.

https://www.ducksters.com/science/earth_science/clouds.php
Read more on how clouds form and move.

http://science.howstuffworks.com/nature/natural-disasters/hurricane.htm
Learn more about hurricanes and the destruction that they cause.

www.kids.nationalgeographic.com/nature/habitats/article/desert
Read about all the different deserts of the world, then watch a fun video.

www.windows2universe.org/sun/sun.html
See more information on the different zones of the Sun and how they work.

www.esa.int/esaKIDSen/Starsandgalaxies.html
Read about supernovas and other ways stars die at the kids' webpages of the European Space Agency.

http://hubblesite.org/explore_astronomy/black_holes/
Watch animated videos and take a visual journey from Earth to two different black holes at the official website of the Hubble Space Telescope.

CHAPTER TWO
PREHISTORIC LIFE

This *Clevosaurus* is a relative of the tuatara, a reptile found in New Zealand today.

Thecodontosaurus's teeth are adapted to slicing through plant stems and leaves. This early dinosaur is about 3.9 to 4.9 ft. (1.2 to 1.5m) in length.

A Thecodontosaurus (top) grazes on plants during the Triassic period (248 to 206 million years ago). Its legs are positioned underneath its body and support its weight. Most other reptiles of the time have legs splayed on either side of their bodies.

DINO TIMELINE

The time of the dinosaurs spanned three time periods. Dinosaurs emerged in the Triassic period, and flourished in the Jurassic and Cretaceous periods. There were many types and species. Those shown on the blue lines were lizard-hipped; those on yellow lines were bird-hipped.

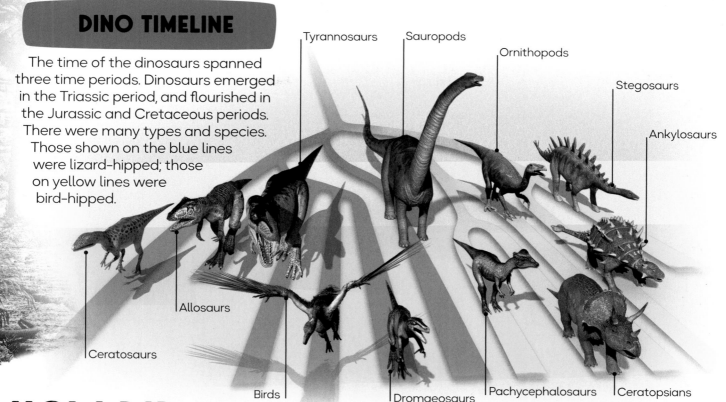

Tyrannosaurs

Sauropods

Ornithopods

Stegosaurs

Ankylosaurs

Ceratosaurs

Allosaurs

Birds

Dromaeosaurs

Pachycephalosaurs

Ceratopsians

HOW DID DINOSAURS EVOLVE?

Dinosaurs were reptiles that lived on land between 230 million years ago and 66 million years ago. During much of that time, they were the dominant land animals on the planet. They evolved from primitive reptiles, known as archosaurs, that lived before them.

Over time, dinosaurs evolved into many different types, ranging in size from small birdlike creatures to enormous four-legged sauropods, the largest of which measured more than 100 ft. (30m) in length and may have weighed as much as 110 tons. As some species of dinosaurs died out, new species emerged. So far, scientists have discovered the remains of more than 1,100 different species of dinosaurs. Although the name dinosaur comes from the Greek for "terrible lizard," many species were gentle plant eaters.

HIP GROUPS

Dinosaurs are grouped by the design of their hip joints. The lizard-hipped ones (saurischians) have a pubis bone that points forward. The bird-hipped ones (ornithischians) have a backward-pointing pubis bone.

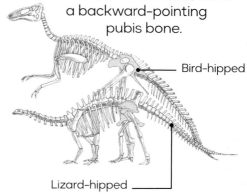

Bird-hipped

Lizard-hipped

FIRST DINOSAURS

Early dinosaurs such as *Pisanosaurus, Eoraptor,* and *Hetereodontosaurus* (pictured) flourished about 230 million years ago. *Hetereodontosaurus* was a slim, lizard-hipped dinosaur, about 3.9 ft. (1.2m) long, that ate plants.

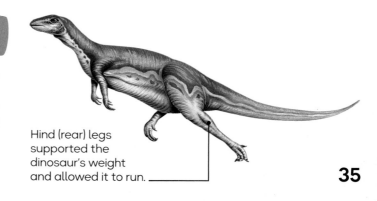

Hind (rear) legs supported the dinosaur's weight and allowed it to run.

HOW DID DINOSAUR FOSSILS FORM?

Fossils are the preserved remains or traces of things that lived in the remote past. Most fossils are found in rocks. Much of what we know about dinosaurs comes from the discovery of their fossilized bones or tracks.

A fossil may be a creature's skeleton, or the preserved remains of the food, droppings, or tracks the creature left behind (trace fossils). Some fossils are remains preserved in ice. Others are preserved in sticky resin that has hardened to form amber. Most dinosaur fossils, however, were created by layer upon layer of sediment building up over a skeleton that, over time, used the hard body parts, such as bones and teeth, to solidify in rock layers. Landslides, erosion, and movements in Earth's crust may bring these layers to the surface, where they can be discovered by scientists.

These fossilized remains, of two dinosaurs dramatically locked in combat, were discovered in the Flaming Cliffs region of the Gobi Desert in Mongolia, in 1971. The box below left, shows what probably occurred.

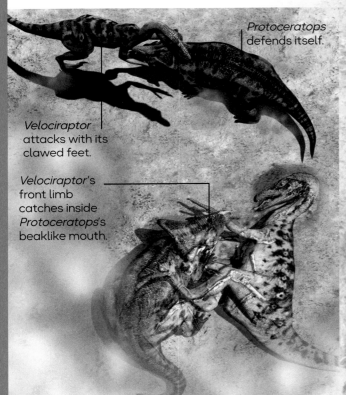

Protoceratops defends itself.

Velociraptor attacks with its clawed feet.

Velociraptor's front limb catches inside *Protoceratops*'s beaklike mouth.

DINOSAUR DUEL

More than 74 million years ago, a *Velociraptor* attacked a plant-eating *Protoceratops*. The *Protoceratops* fought back, but then a collapsing cliff or a sandstorm covered the creatures in sediment, and their remains began to fossilize.

The long tail of *Protoceratops* is made up of separate bone segments.

The large upper leg bone of *Protoceratops* is preserved in the desert rock.

36

Velociraptor's lightweight skull is filled with large, sharp teeth.

Neck bones of *Velociraptor*. The dinosaur is about 6 to 6.6 ft. (1.8 to 2m) long.

Velociraptor's leg ends in a foot armed with a large, sickle-shaped claw for slashing prey.

FOSSILIZATION

Layers of sediment on top of a dinosaur skeleton mount, pressure builds, and the sediment hardens. Minerals from the sediment fill the skeleton, preserving the shape of the bones.

1. Dinosaur dies and soft body parts begin to decompose (rot away).

2. Remains are covered in layers of sand, mud, or other sediment.

3. Fossilization occurs as layers of sediment harden into rock.

4. Rock layers above are eroded to bring fossil skeleton to the surface.

SEALED IN CAVES

Some fossil deposits of dinosaurs have been found surrounded by strata (layers) of much earlier rock. This is because the dinosaur may have fallen or been washed away into deep caves.

1. Dinosaur grazes on plants close to limestone depressions and caves.

2. Dinosaur dies and its body is washed away by rains or floods into the cave.

3. Layers of sediment build up over the bones to create fossils (see box above).

HOW DO WE KNOW ABOUT DINOSAURS?

The fossil record has taught us much about the size, structure, and habits of dinosaurs. Making new fossil discoveries, and further investigating those already made, helps experts learn more about how dinosaurs lived and died.

Paleontology is the scientific study of prehistoric life. It includes a range of different subjects, from geology to biology and computer science. Some paleontologists specialize in studying one particular dinosaur or one fossil type, such as teeth or fossilized plants. Others concentrate on seeking out fossil beds that may yield important new finds. Fossils have to be identified and some experts use scanning microscopes and other new technologies to examine them in great detail. Wear marks on teeth and jaw bones, for example, can provide important information about how and what a dinosaur ate.

In 1947, U.S. paleontologist Edwin H. Colbert discovered more than 100 Coelophysis skeletons at Ghost Ranch in New Mexico. These early dinosaurs lived about 210 million years ago. The group may have been killed suddenly by a flash flood.

Skull has large eye sockets, so scientists think that *Coelophysis* had good eyesight.

A large adult *Coelophysis* stood about 3 ft. (1m) tall at the hip.

Small, pointed head with mouth containing about 80 small, sharp teeth for tearing at flesh.

DIGGING DEEP

Paleontologists unearth the fossilized skeleton of an *Edmontosaurus* at Hell Creek in North Dakota. The bones have to be cleaned carefully, cataloged, and then compared with others to confirm the dinosaur type.

Mandible
(lower jaw)

Long neck made
of many individual
vertebrae bones.

Three-toed foot.

BONE JIGSAW

Skeletons are rarely found whole,
so much detective work has to be
done to piece the parts together.
Sometimes "complete" skeletons on
display in museums use bones from
different skeletons.

Long tail keeps the
dinosaur balanced
and agile as it runs.

Large leg bones are
hollow, for lightness
and speed.

3-D MODELING

Some scientists use computers to create
3-D models of dinosaur skeletons. These
help them study dinosaur body parts and
see how they may have moved and worked.

HOW DID MARINE REPTILES LIVE DURING THE DINOSAUR AGE?

Dinosaurs were reptiles that lived on land, although occasionally some did venture into water. Marine reptiles existed at the same time as the dinosaurs and lived their entire lives in the seas and oceans.

The waters of Earth's prehistoric seas were teeming with fish, squidlike animals, and creatures with hard shells such as ammonites. Large marine reptiles such as plesiosaurs, nathosaurs, and ichthyosaurs would hunt these animals with powerful jaws, crushing the shells and spines and swallowing the prey whole. Some of these predators became prey themselves for the largest, most ferocious marine reptiles such as *Liopleurodon*. Marine reptiles did not have gills like fish so they needed to surface to breathe air.

More than 150 million years ago, plesiosaurs swam the Jurassic seas in search of prey. These large marine reptiles had broad, shallow bodies with long necks, and typically grew to about 11.5 ft. (3.5m) in length.

Plesiosaurs "fly" through the water by flapping their two pairs of flippers alternately.

ICHTHYOSAURS

These sharklike marine reptiles had long, slim jaws lined with many sharp teeth for catching fish and mollusks. Large eyes may have helped them hunt in murky waters. One species of ichthyosaur, *Temnodontosaurus*, had gigantic eyes—each at least 8 in. (20cm) wide.

A long, flexible spine ended in a gristly tail that would beat back and forth to move through water.

Large eye socket

Small hind fins may have helped keep the reptile balanced in the water.

Elasmosaurus was a marine reptile that lived about 80 million years ago, mostly near the water's surface. It possessed one of the longest necks of any known marine reptile. The neck measured between 16 and 21 ft. (5 and 6.5m) long and was made up of more than 70 vertebrae.

Nostrils on top of head to breathe air when surfacing.

Long, flexible neck swings back and forth through schools of fish when hunting.

Sharp, cone-shaped teeth line the jaw, allowing plesiosaurs to rip and tear prey.

Powerful jaw muscles generated huge crushing forces.

PLIOSAURS

Thrust upward by the force of its muscular flippers, a *pliosaur* catches an ichthyosaur in its fearsome jaws. One of the largest pliosaur skulls ever found—off the coast of Dorset, England, in 2008—measured 7.9 ft. (2.4m) in length.

HOW DID PREHISTORIC REPTILES FLY?

Flying reptiles, known as pterosaurs, soared through the skies in prehistoric times. Most pterosaurs were fairly small but some Cretaceous species were enormous. Close relatives of the dinosaurs, they possessed lightweight bodies and wings made of living tissue rather than feathers.

Pterosaurs may have been clumsy on land, walking on all fours and using the claws on their wings to crawl. They were more agile in the air, using their wings to glide on air currents and their keen eyesight and long beaks to seek out food to catch and eat. Some species had an area of tissue between their rear legs, which formed an extra wing called an uropatagium.

Three different species of pterosaurs glide above the Solnhofen lagoon. This is now a region in southern Germany—an area rich in pterosaur fossils.

Large eyes are used for detecting prey.

Rhamphorhynchus's arm ends in four fingerlike digits. The first three form a claw while the very long fourth digit extends along the front edge of the wing.

A *Ctenochasma* flies low to the ground. Adult *Ctenochasma* had as many as 400 teeth in their long beaks.

IN FLIGHT

Scientists are still learning about pterosaurs and flight. This model shows how a large pterosaur may have flown. Its giant wings are attached to its arms and body and are made of thin layers of a strong, leathery membrane.

1. The pterosaur keeps its wings largely still as it soars on warm, rising air.

2. Powerful muscles attached to its body pull its arms and wings downward, and then push upward.

3. As the wings move up and down, their curve may alter in shape, generating some extra lift.

42

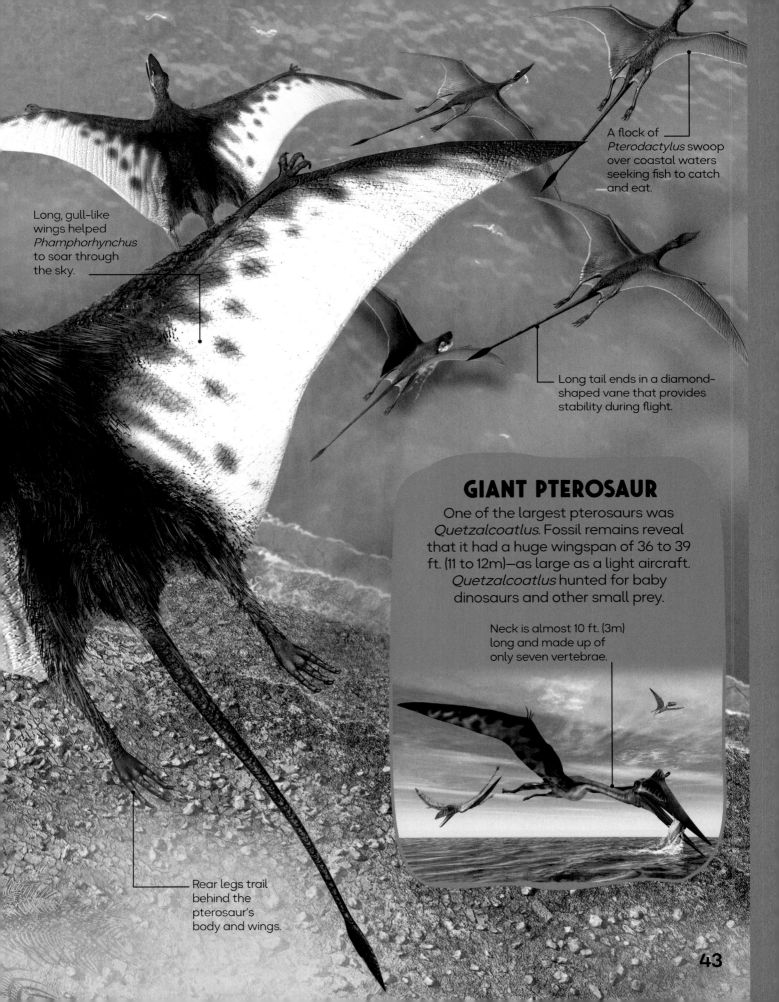

A flock of _Pterodactylus_ swoop over coastal waters seeking fish to catch and eat.

Long, gull-like wings helped _Phamphorhynchus_ to soar through the sky.

Long tail ends in a diamond-shaped vane that provides stability during flight.

GIANT PTEROSAUR

One of the largest pterosaurs was _Quetzalcoatlus_. Fossil remains reveal that it had a huge wingspan of 36 to 39 ft. (11 to 12m)—as large as a light aircraft. _Quetzalcoatlus_ hunted for baby dinosaurs and other small prey.

Neck is almost 10 ft. (3m) long and made up of only seven vertebrae.

Rear legs trail behind the pterosaur's body and wings.

HOW DID DINOSAURS WALK AND RUN?

Dinosaurs varied greatly in size and weight but they all relied on large muscles attached to their leg and hip bones for movement. Stretches of tough, fibrous tissue called tendons connected the muscles to the bones. The muscles contracted and relaxed to move their legs.

Some dinosaurs were bipeds, meaning that they walked on two legs. Others, like *Iguanadon,* could walk on all fours or on two legs. Smaller bipeds, such as *Gallimimus* and *Eoraptor,* were lightly built, swift runners. However, the giant four-legged sauropods, such as *Apatosaurus* and *Diplodocus,* moved far more slowly. Fossilized footprints show that they would stride forward with one front leg and a rear leg on the opposite side, then take their next step with their other two legs moving forward.

Eoraptor, an early dinosaur, runs on two legs to catch a small lizard. Relatively small at 3 ft. (1m) long, and nimble, Eoraptor uses its speed both to hunt and to outrun other predators.

Eoraptor is an omnivore—it eats both animals and plants.

Good eyesight allows *Eoraptor* to hunt small, fast-moving prey.

Jaw is fitted with both carnivore and herbivore types of teeth—some sharp for slicing; some blunt for grinding.

BONE DETECTIVES

Fossilized skeletons offer paleontologists important clues about how dinosaurs may have moved. These are often compared with the movements of creatures alive today that have similar skeletons.

Tail may have been used to help dinosaur balance as it changed direction.

Leg structure enables scientists to guess the length of its stride.

Foot design shows that this dinosaur is a digitigrade—a creature that runs on its toes.

Heavy tail helped balance the weight of the dinosaur's head.

FAST PREDATOR

A large, predatory dinosaur from Mongolia, *Tarbosaurus* moved quickly over short distances and used its enormous, 4.3-ft. (1.3-m) -long head as a battering ram when attacking prey.

Small arms for grappling with prey.

Large, powerful rear legs. *Tarbosaurus* stood about 12.5 ft. (3.8m) tall at its hips.

Hip joint connects upper leg bone to dinosaur's spine.

Tail bones

Tail acts as a counterweight balancing the forward tilt of *Eoraptor*'s neck and body.

TRACKS

Series of fossilized footprints have left behind "dino highways" for paleontologists to study. These can reveal a lot about different dinosaurs' running speeds, stride lengths, and movement.

Strong upper leg and hip muscles generate the power for quick movement.

Gallimimus may have sprinted at speeds of up to 50 mph (80km/h).

Apatosaurus covered about 16.5 ft. (5m) each time one of its legs took a stride.

Eoraptor walks and runs on its front three toes.

Hinge joint allows dinosaur to tilt its foot up or down.

Rear legs of *Dryosaurus* left prints in drying mud.

SAUROPODS IN SCALE

Sauropods varied greatly in size. The smallest were 20 to 23 ft. (6 to 7m) long; the largest up to 115 ft. (35m) long. Here are six giant sauropod species.

1. *Supersaurus*
2. *Bruhathkayosaurus*
3. *Amphicoelias*
4. *Sauroposeidon*
5. *Argentinosaurus*
6. *Dreadnoughtus*

Brachiosaurus's chisel-shaped teeth strip branches of leaves.

About 160 million years ago, herds of Brachiosaurus crash through foliage, feeding on tree leaves. With long front legs, these animals stand 39 ft. (12m) tall and can strip leaves off trees taller than other plant eaters.

LIVING TOGETHER

Scientists believe that different types of sauropods grazed together in the same areas. Taller sauropods feasted on leaves high up in the treetops, leaving the leaves of smaller trees and plants for the shorter sauropods to eat.

Diplodocus grew to 108 ft. (33m) in length.

An average *Camarasaurus* was 49 ft. (15m) long.

A younger *Brachiosaurus* rears up to reach araucaria tree leaves.

HOW DID SAUROPODS SURVIVE?

Sauropods were the largest animals ever to have walked on Earth. The heaviest weighed more than 110 tons. Equipped with four stout legs, a long neck, and a long tail, these plant-eating giants had to graze constantly in order to survive.

The sauropods' sheer size made them hard to attack. Most had a small head perched on a long neck to give them a wide feeding range from one position. Food was not chewed, but swallowed and digested in the body with the help of swallowed stones to pulp the food. Despite their slow movement and lack of defenses, sauropods flourished. Their fossils have been found on every continent, including Antarctica.

Neck skeleton is made up of a series of vertebrae bones.

Gizzard contains swallowed stones that pulp and grind up food.

Huge thigh bones help support the dinosaur's weight of about 10 tons.

Large lungs help fill sauropod's blood with oxygen.

SAUROPOD STRUCTURE

Because so little of a dinosaur's soft tissue is ever fossilized, scientists make guesses about what the inside of a sauropod looked like. This diagram shows a *Rapetosaurus*, one of a group of titanosaurian sauropods that were among the last to exist— up until about 66 million years ago.

Giant stomach where plants are partially digested.

47

BETTER TOGETHER

Parasaurolophus were a species of hadrosaur that lived in the late Cretaceous period. Paleontologists have found large numbers of hadrosaur fossils in the same location, suggesting they lived in herds. Sometimes fossils from multiple species are found together, meaning different hadrosaurs may have coexisted peacefully.

HOW DID DINOSAURS LIVE TOGETHER IN HERDS?

Large numbers of the same species of dinosaurs have been found together in fossil sites known as bone beds. A herd of *Styracosaurs* was found in a bone bed in Arizona, for example. Living in a large, moving herd made it harder for predators to single out an individual.

Other evidence for dinosaur herds comes from large groups of fossil footprints known as trackways, and from the discovery of nesting sites with many fossilized eggs. Some herds may have been temporary, such as when dinosaurs gathered at a water hole, but many dinosaurs lived in herds all their lives. Herds provided partners to mate with, help with raising young, and offered protection from attack by predators.

Adult *Iguanodon* running with head held low.

Young *Iguanodon* running alongside the adults.

PACK SAFETY

This picture shows a herd of *Iguanodon* fleeing an attack from the fast, predatory dinosaur *Deinonychus*. Adult *Iguanodon* positioned themselves at the front and rear of the group to protect their young in the middle of the pack.

A herd of Iguanodon graze at the shoreline in the early Cretaceous period. The young dinosaurs stay close to their parents as they rest and eat, while the elder dinosaurs keep a lookout for any signs of danger.

Struthiomimus may have been an omnivore, eating lizards as well as plants. When threatened with attack from larger predators, however, its powerful legs helped it sprint to safety at speeds of 50 mph (80km/h) or more.

HOW DID DINOSAURS DEFEND THEMSELVES?

Some dinosaurs escaped predators by camouflaging themselves, or by using their speed to evade capture. Others possessed heavy body armor or body parts specialized to fend off attacks.

We do not know how dinosaur skin was colored, but it is likely that some dinosaurs could conceal themselves in forests or undergrowth using their skin color as camouflage. Others did not need camouflage because they had thick armor for protection. *Protoceratops* and *Triceratops* had a bony frill around their head that helped protect their neck from attack. Others, such as *Ankylosaurus,* had a body covered in tough plates, making them hard to injure. Attacked dinosaurs may have used the claws on their feet to fight back or they may have lashed out with their tail.

Bony plates are covered in horny knobs and spikes called osteoderms.

DINO ARMOR

Stegosaurus was a heavyset dinosaur living about 150 million years ago. The large, bony plates running along its back may have been there for show but may also have protected it from attack by making it look larger than it really was.

Largest bony plates were about 24 in. (60cm) high and 24 in. (60cm) wide.

Strong tail armed with four spikes was a powerful defensive weapon.

Ankylosaurus's club may have weighed more than 110 lb. (50kg).

A large meat eater, Albertosaurus, attacks a plant eater, Ankylosaurus, which fights back using its armored tail. The tail ends in a heavy club made of bone. A powerful swing could bash the attacker's body with enough force to break bones.

HAND AND FOOT SPURS

Some species of dinosaurs had sharp spikes or horns on their feet known as spurs. These may have been used to stab or slash an enemy when attacked. This *Iguanodon* had a large, pointed spike in the thumb position on each hand.

HOW DID *TYRANNOSAURUS* HUNT AND KILL PREY?

Tyrannosaurus rex—or *T. rex*—is the most famous dinosaur of all. This fearsome meat eater was one of the largest land carnivores, growing up to 41 ft. (12.5m) long and weighing 8 to 9 tons. It was also one of the last dinosaurs to become extinct.

Scientists used to debate whether *Tyrannosaurus rex* was a pure scavenger, but it is now certain it was a ferocious killer. Armed with immense jaws and bone-crushing teeth, it could probably kill any animal it encountered. Its arms, though small, were very muscular, and its hands—ending in two sharp claws—helped it to grip prey at close quarters. Studies have shown this predator had a remarkable sense of smell, allowing it to sniff out and stalk its prey.

IN FOR THE KILL

This sequence shows one way in which *Tyrannosaurus rex* may have attacked and killed a duck-billed dinosaur named *Anatotitan*.

1. *T-rex* stalks its prey, a herd of *Anatotitan* that is trapped in a forest clearing.

2. One animal is singled out and circled before *T-rex* lunges and clamps its massive jaws on the prey's neck.

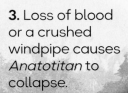

3. Loss of blood or a crushed windpipe causes *Anatotitan* to collapse.

Jaw and neck muscles were so strong that this dinosaur could kill by shaking its victims apart.

BIG BITE

Here, a *T-rex* is shown feasting on its prey. A blunt snout, powerful jaws and 12-in. (30-cm) -long teeth enabled it to slice and tear away flesh, possibly as much as 165 lb. (75kg) of meat in a single bite.

Duck-billed *Corythosaurus* is a plant eater that measures up to 33 ft. (10m) long.

Forward-facing eyes are about 3 in. (7cm) in diameter, allowing *T-rex* to judge depth and distance.

Large nostril openings

BIG SKULL

Tyrannosaurus rex's giant skull measured up to 5 ft. (1.5m) long and featured incredibly powerful jaws. Its 60 daggerlike teeth were strong enough to crunch through bone or the heavy armor of its prey. To reduce its weight, the skull had large openings called fenestrae.

Stiff tail is used for balance and helps *T.rex* to "steer" as it moves.

Powerful hind legs support the dinosaur's heavy weight.

*A **Tyrannosaurus** attacks a group of **Corythosaurus** in late Cretaceous North America. It is not certain how fast Tyrannosaurus rex could run, but it would have charged swiftly as it attacked its prey*.

HOW DID DINOSAURS HUNT IN PACKS?

Some dinosaurs may have worked together in packs to bring down and kill their prey. Paleontologists have discovered the bones of small predatory dinosaurs, such as *Deinonychus*, in one site. Recent evidence suggests that large predators such as *Tyrannosaurus* may also have hunted in packs.

Smaller predators, such as *Deinonychus*, may have worked together in intelligent groups, communicating with one another as they stalked their prey. While not hunting specifically together, *Velociraptor* may have taken turns to leap on the back of their prey, biting, and slashing with their claws.

A giant Argentinosaurus is too large for a single Giganotosaurus to bring down and they may have worked together as a pack to attack the sauropod repeatedly.

Giganotosaurus may have weighed 8 to 10 tons—more than a *Tyrannosaurus rex.*

LIGHTWEIGHT KILLER

Velociraptor's skull was about 10 in. (25cm) long. It was light in weight and had serrated teeth suited to tearing away small amounts of flesh. *Velociraptor* was too small to bring down large prey by itself, so some scientists believe this dinosaur may hunted in packs.

PACK ATTACK

A group of *Deinonychus* is shown here savaging a *Tenontosaurus* in a forest during the Cretaceous period. Two jumped on the animal's back while a third attacked its neck. *Deinonychus* had huge claws on its second toes. It used these to slash and tear its prey.

Attacker takes a bite while clawing its victim's flank with its sharp claws.

Argentinosaurus measures more than 82 ft. (25m) in length and weighs 66 to 83 tons.

Giganotosaurus attacks the neck area, aiming to cut major arteries.

HOW DID DINOSAURS SEE, SMELL, TASTE, AND HEAR?

Studying dinosaurs' senses is difficult because so little evidence of their eyes and other sense organs remains. However, experts believe that dinosaurs were equipped with sense organs remarkably similar to those found in animals today.

Vision may have been many dinosaurs' most important sense. Some would have had a wide field of vision that allowed them to see in almost all directions without moving their head—vital for spotting signs of danger. Others, particularly predators, had binocular vision in which the eyes' field of vision overlapped. This enabled them to judge distances to objects accurately. The sense of smell was important, too, for sniffing out prey, particular plants to eat, or a mate to breed with. Taste was probably the weakest of most dinosaurs' senses.

HIGH AND LOW

Different types of dinosaurs could probably hear different frequencies of sounds. This is similar to the way in which large modern birds can hear low-pitched sounds better than small birds can. Small birds are better at hearing high-pitched sounds.

Hearing detects low-pitched thuds of a large dinosaur's approaching footsteps..

Head rears up so that eyes can search for signs of approaching danger.

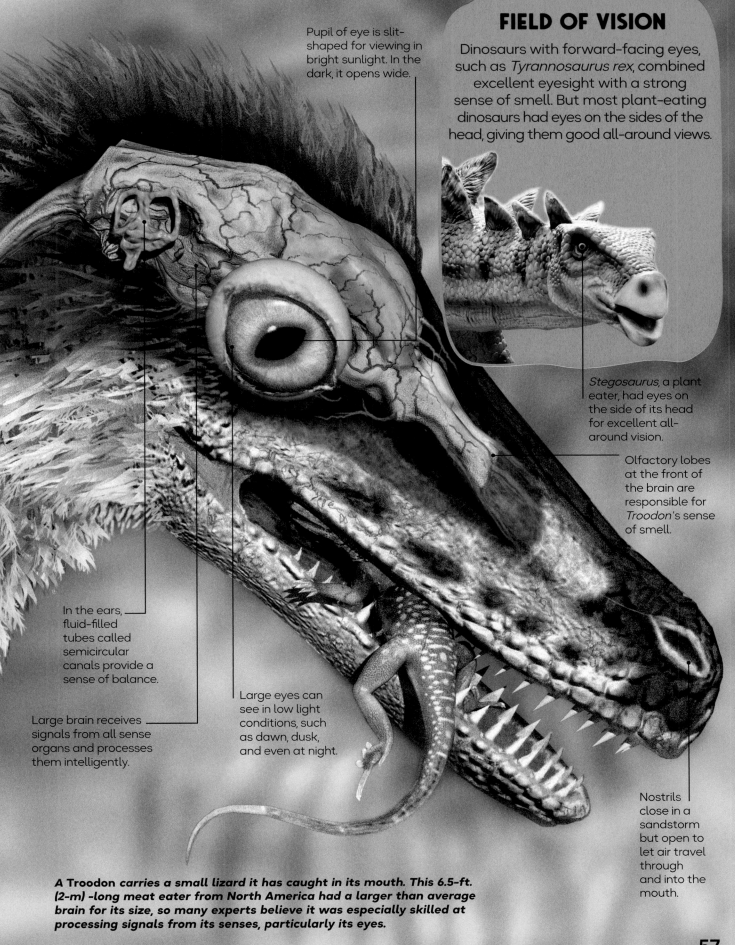

Pupil of eye is slit-shaped for viewing in bright sunlight. In the dark, it opens wide.

FIELD OF VISION

Dinosaurs with forward-facing eyes, such as *Tyrannosaurus rex*, combined excellent eyesight with a strong sense of smell. But most plant-eating dinosaurs had eyes on the sides of the head, giving them good all-around views.

Stegosaurus, a plant eater, had eyes on the side of its head for excellent all-around vision.

Olfactory lobes at the front of the brain are responsible for *Troodon*'s sense of smell.

In the ears, fluid-filled tubes called semicircular canals provide a sense of balance.

Large eyes can see in low light conditions, such as dawn, dusk, and even at night.

Large brain receives signals from all sense organs and processes them intelligently.

Nostrils close in a sandstorm but open to let air travel through and into the mouth.

A Troodon *carries a small lizard it has caught in its mouth. This 6.5-ft. (2-m) -long meat eater from North America had a larger than average brain for its size, so many experts believe it was especially skilled at processing signals from its senses, particularly its eyes.*

57

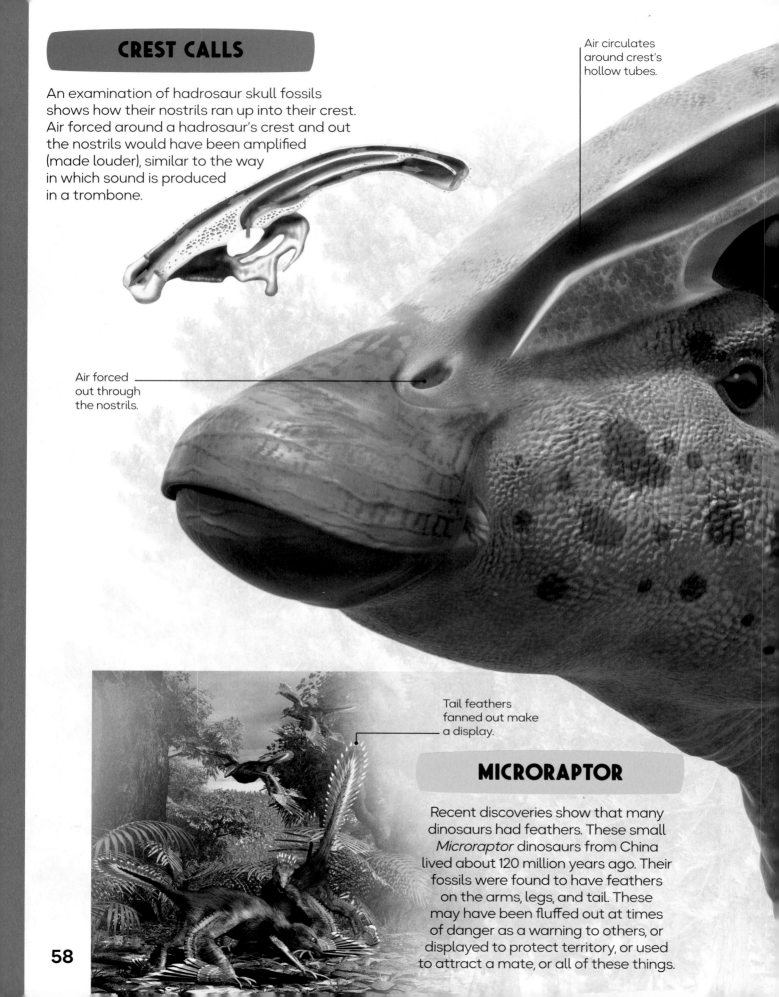

CREST CALLS

An examination of hadrosaur skull fossils shows how their nostrils ran up into their crest. Air forced around a hadrosaur's crest and out the nostrils would have been amplified (made louder), similar to the way in which sound is produced in a trombone.

Air circulates around crest's hollow tubes.

Air forced out through the nostrils.

Tail feathers fanned out make a display.

MICRORAPTOR

Recent discoveries show that many dinosaurs had feathers. These small *Microraptor* dinosaurs from China lived about 120 million years ago. Their fossils were found to have feathers on the arms, legs, and tail. These may have been fluffed out at times of danger as a warning to others, or displayed to protect territory, or used to attract a mate, or all of these things.

Diplodocus had a very long tail made up of more than 70 bony vertebrae, which it may have cracked like a whip to make an extremely loud sound. This may have scared off predators, and helped *Diplodocus* keep in contact with its herd over long distances.

Crest made of bone with hollow passages throughout.

Tail tapers so that it was slender along much of its length.

HOW DID DINOSAURS COMMUNICATE?

The dinosaur age was far from silent. The thuds of giant footsteps and the cries and crashes of battling dinosaurs may have mixed with the roars and mating calls of others. Dinosaurs may also have used visual signals to communicate.

We cannot be certain what dinosaurs sounded like, but we can be fairly sure that they made noises. Judging by the size of some dinosaurs' lungs, many of these noises may have been extremely loud. Certain duck-billed dinosaurs, known as hadrosaurs, all had large, bony crests on the top of their head through which air may have circulated to produce loud, trumpeting sounds. Dinosaurs may also have used visual displays or body language—such as foot stamping, rearing up, or shaking their head when trying to attract a mate or defend territory from others in the herd.

Parasaurolophus was a hadrosaur with an enormous head crest that curved backward from its head. This may have allowed it to produce a bellow loud enough to be heard over great distances.

HOW WERE DINOSAURS BORN?

Major fossil finds show that dinosaurs laid eggs, just as birds, fish, and reptiles do today. Fossilized dinosaur eggs have been found in hundreds of sites throughout the world. Most are around 4 to 8 in. (10 to 20cm) long.

The egg, laid in a nest in the ground, provided a food source for the dinosaur embryo as it developed. The shell protected the embryo and was broken by the baby dinosaur's beak or claws when it was ready to hatch. Some newly hatched dinosaurs were able to walk and eat as soon as they were born. Other species needed to be taken care of. The worn teeth of fossilized baby dinosaurs, found in nests, show that they were brought food—small leaves, seeds, and berries—by their parents, who would also ave protected them from small, fast predators.

A group of Maiasaura rear their young. Babies hatch from eggs laid in circular nests. As many as 40 eggs are laid in a single nest. Maiasaura nests found in Montana were repaired, suggesting that the dinosaurs returned to the same nesting sites to lay their eggs.

MOTHER AND YOUNG

A group of infant dinosaurs, no more than a year old, are shown here huddling around their mother. Among the fossil remains of dinosaurs, including *Psittacosaurus* and *Maiasaura*, young dinosaurs have been found close to adults that were probably their parents.

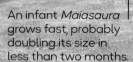

An infant *Maiasaura* grows fast, probably doubling its size in less than two months.

Two young *Maiasaura* stay near their mother.

COVERED NEST

Some dinosaurs scratched a hole in the ground to lay their eggs. They then covered the eggs with loose soil, leaves, and other plant matter to protect the eggs and help keep them warm.

Eggs protected in hollow.

Layers of plant matter and soil form mound.

Female keeps her eggs warm by laying her stomach over the nest.

INSIDE THE EGG

This shows a *Maiasaura* baby curled up inside its egg, which was about the size of an ostrich egg. When the baby hatched, it was about 20 in. (50cm) long and grew into an adult of about 30 ft. (9m) in length.

A rocky object from space struck Earth in the Yucatán Peninsula in present-day Mexico. The resulting Chicxulub crater, almost 125 mi. (200km) in diameter, was discovered only in the 1970s, buried under new rocks formed since the impact.

Meteorite was destroyed upon impact.

HOW DID THE DINOSAURS DIE OUT?

After flourishing for more than 160 million years, dinosaurs, large marine reptiles, and many other creatures were suddenly wiped out. Most scientists think that this mass extinction was caused by a massive meteorite impact.

About 66 million years ago, a large meteorite, at least 6 mi. (10 km) in diameter, is thought to have struck Earth. The resulting blast, more powerful than two million atomic bombs, generated intense heat, giant tsunami waves, and vast clouds of dust. These clouds blotted out sunlight, plunging the world into cold and darkness, possibly for many years. Dinosaurs were unable to survive the devastation and the floods or the extreme change in climate and lack of food that followed, as many plant species were wiped out, too. However, some creaturesdid survive, including early birds, many insects, and small mammal species.

Alamosaurus is one of the last sauropods.

SURVIVORS

Dinosaurs didn't completely die out. Early birds evolved from small, feathered theropods—and modern birds can be seen as living dinosaurs.

Today, there are more than 10,000 species of birds.

NEW SPECIES

Over time, new species of creatures evolved. *Nimravidae*, a species of saber-toothed cat, flourished more than 20 million years after the dinosaurs died out. A large, predatory mammal, it too became extinct about seven million years ago.

Large dinosaurs, such as this *Tyrannosaurus rex*, will be wiped out.

Dinosaurs flee in terror from the intense heat and dust caused by the meteorite impact. Species that cannot cope with the new climate conditions will quickly become extinct.

Triceratops is among the last of the ceratopsians.

PREHISTORIC LIFE
FIND OUT MORE ABOUT HOW THE WORLD WORKS

WEBSITES TO VISIT

www.kids-dinosaurs.com
Learn more about all kinds of dinosaurs and how they lived at this colorful website.

www.dinohunters.com/index.htm
Find out who discovered which dinosaurs first and read short profiles of famous fossil finders, including Mary Anning and Gideon Mantell.

www.nhm.ac..uk/discover/dino-directory.html
Check out the details of more than 300 dinosaur species at this Dino Directory created by the Natural History Museum, London, U.K.

www.sciencekids.co.nz/sciencefacts/dinosaurs.html
Here you will find key facts and images on a wide range of different dinosaurs.

www.amnh.org/explore/ology/paleontology
Learn all about what palaeontology involves and find out information from real-life palaeontologists.

www.newscientist.com/article/dn9919-instant-expert-dinosaurs.html
Check out New Scientist magazine's introductory guide to dinosaurs and how they lived. The web pages also include the latest news on dinosaur finds.

www.ucmp.berkeley.edu/diapsids/saurischia/tyrannosauridae.html
Learn more about Tyrannosaurus rex and see how a skeleton is prepared for display.

www.discoveringfossils.co.uk/whatisafossil.htm
Read more about how fossils are made and view many famous fossil-hunting sites around Great Britain in this website's resources section.

www.plesiosauria.com/index.php
Learn about different plesiosaur species and how they lived and moved at the website of marine reptile researcher Dr. Adam Stuart Smith.

http://science.nationalgeographic.com/science/prehistoric-world/mass-extinction/
Read about mass extinctions in Earth's past, then view the galleries of dinosaurs and fossils found on the National Geographic website.

CHAPTER THREE
LIFE

Some rainforest trees grow to great heights in order to compete for light.

Chloroplasts contain the substance chlorophyll, which absorbs energy from sunlight. This produces a chemical reaction with water (drawn up by the plant's roots) and carbon dioxide gas (taken in from the air) to produce oxygen and glucose.

Sunlight reaches the leaf, where chlorophyll aborbs the light's energy.

Carbon dioxide is absorbed by the leaves through tiny pores called stoma.

Oxygen is released from leaves through the stoma.

Water, carbon dioxide, and the energy from sunlight react inside chloroplasts to generate sugars and oxygen.

Glucose is either moved around the plant or stored as food.

HOW DO PLANTS GROW?

Plants need sunlight, water, air, and soil to grow. Most species of plants make their food for growth through a process known as photosynthesis. This takes place in chloroplasts (specialized cells) inside the plant's leaves.

Photosynthesis creates energy-rich sugars that are transported around the plant as food or are made into more complex chemicals and stored inside the plant. These chemicals include cellulose, which is used to build new cell walls when the plant's cells grow and divide as it grows bigger. If a young plant continues to get the correct nutrients and the correct conditions for it to photosynthesize, it will grow into a mature plant. A few plants do not get everything they need from photosynthesis or from the soil. Some, such as the Venus flytrap and bladderworts, digest insects to gain nutrients. Others, such as ivy and orchids, are parasites—they grow upon, and take nutrients from, other plants.

A tropical rainforest is dense with trees and plant life, most seeking out sunlight to help fuel their growth. Below the main canopy of tall trees lies an understory that receives less sunlight. As a result, plants in the understory tend to be smaller but with larger leaves to catch sunlight.

GROWING FROM A SEED

When the conditions are right, a plant seed may start to grow. At first, it uses its food store within the seed, but as it grows leaves, which open to catch sunlight, it can start making food through photosynthesis. Its roots draw in water and nutrients from the soil.

1. The seed coating splits and a root starts to grow downward.

2. The root develops rootlets that branch off and grow into the soil.

3. A stem emerges and begins to grow upward.

4. The plant grows its first large leaves supported on its stem.

ASEXUAL REPRODUCTION

Some bacteria reproduce asexually by simply splitting themselves in two. This process is known as binary fission. Each offspring is an exact genetic copy of its parent.

Single bacterium

Cell grows and starts to divide into two

Two daughter cells created

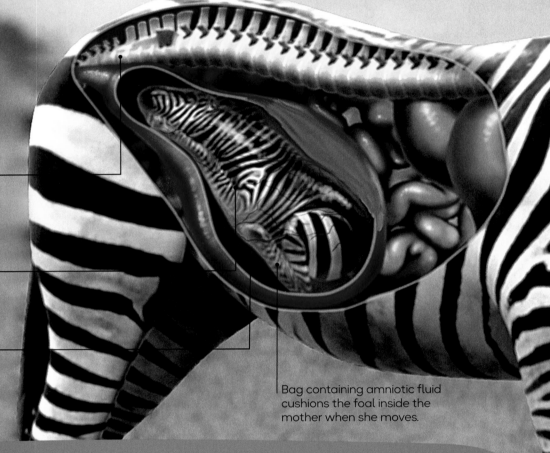

Backbone must support extra weight of foal and fluid carried by the female zebra.

Foal will be able to stand and suckle milk from its mother shortly after it is born.

Foal receives nourishment from the placenta—an organ connected to the side of the uterus.

Bag containing amniotic fluid cushions the foal inside the mother when she moves.

EMBRYO GROWTH

Nurtured and kept warm inside a fluid-filled sac, and protected by the wall of the uterus, the tiny human embryo (as it is known at first) rapidly grows. It soon becomes a recognizably human fetus and reaches full size after about 40 weeks.

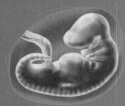

1. Embryo after six weeks

2. Embryo after eight weeks, now known as a fetus

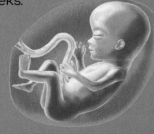

3. Umbilical cord supplies nutrients to the fetus.

HOW DO CREATURES REPRODUCE?

Reproduction is the creation of offspring—a creature born from existing creatures. In some animals, reproduction takes place with just one parent (asexual), but in others, including humans, it takes place with two parents (sexual).

Asexual reproduction occurs in a number of ways, including budding, found in corals and hydra, where an offspring grows out of the body of the parent. The offspring will be identical to its parent. Sexual reproduction involves specialized sex cells from two parents, most commonly an egg from the female that is fertilized by male sex cells. The offspring will share characteristics of both of its parents but will not be identical to either. Fertilization and development may occur outside the body of the parents or, as in most mammals, the mother may carry the developing young inside her until they are ready to be born live.

LAYING EGGS

Insects, birds, amphibians, most fish, and monotremes—egg-laying mammals such as the echidna and duck-billed platypus— all lay eggs. Inside an egg, a young creature develops. It is nourished and protected until it hatches.

Female fish may lay thousands of eggs at a time.

Female zebra, called a mare, may be just three years old when she has her first foal.

69

BUILDING A DAM

Beavers work at night, quickly carrying mud and stones with their forepaws and timber between their teeth.

Some sticks pushed into streambed

1. The beaver begins the dam by laying sticks, branches, and rocks on the streambed. Logs and larger branches are floated into place.

2. Twigs, stones, and other materials are laid in front of and around the first rows of sticks to build up the dam's height.

Beaver applies and pats down mud using tail.

Dam breaks water's surface, holding back the stream.

3. Mud and clay are pushed up to the dam. This helps stick everything together. When the mixture dries, it makes the dam watertight.

HOW DO BEAVERS BUILD A LODGE

Beavers are plant-eating mammals with extraordinary abilities as home builders. They erect dams across streams to create a pond of still water in which they store food and build their homes, called lodges.

Beavers have poor eyesight, but sharp senses of hearing, smell, and touch. They are most comfortable in water and use their remarkably strong teeth to chop and gnaw wood for food and for building materials. Both their dams and lodges are made of branches and sticks carefully piled together and sealed with mud applied by the beaver's large, flat tail. Their tail is also used as a rudder when swimming, to prop the beaver upright when gnawing wood and to signal an alarm over long distances by slapping it hard on the water's surface.

A family of beavers gathers branches close to their lodge. Beavers mostly eat bark, buds, and wood from trees such as the poplar, birch, or willow. In the summer, they add water plants, berries, and fruit to their diet.

A beaver's dense fur is made waterproof by a thick oil secreted from near its tail.

INSIDE THE LODGE

A lodge provides beavers with a safe winter retreat with entrances out of sight of most predators. A pair of beavers can build a lodge in just a week. Some lodges are repaired and added to by beaver families and may last 30 years or more.

Entrance to the lodge is hidden underwater and near the pond bed.

Lodge made of rocks, sticks, and branches is sealed with an outer covering of mud.

Beavers live in a small room above the water's surface.

Beavers can gnaw and chew through tree trunks up to 10 in. (25cm) in diameter.

Beavers' large, chisel-edged front teeth grow throughout their lives.

A beaver's lodge is built as an island of sticks and mud in the middle of a still pond of water.

An adult beaver can grow to 4.3 ft. (1.3m) long (including its tail) and weigh up to 60 lb. (27kg).

HOW DO CREATURES WORK TOGETHER?

Many creatures of the same species live in large social groups, herds or colonies. They build homes, care for the young, and seek out food together. Sometimes, different species of living things work together so that both benefit in a variety of ways.

Many creatures find that living together in large numbers offers them the greatest chance of survival. Occasionally, two different species offer each other protection in different ways. Clownfish, for example, are covered in a special slimy mucus that allows them to live within the stinging tentacles of sea anemones. These protect the clownfish from predators. In return, clownfish chase away creatures that might feed on sea anemones. Some species offer food to another species in return for a service, such as cleaning or flossing, or, in the case of many plants, dispersing their seeds so that new plants can grow away from the parent plant.

MEERKAT MOB

Meerkats live underground in large social groups called mobs. They come to the surface to forage for insects, small lizards, and other food to eat while members of the group act as sentries on the lookout for danger.

Meerkat adult and infant dig down to uncover a scorpion.

Sentries keep watch for predators coming from different directions.

Antbirds perch on a branch above, waiting to catch any insects fleeing the army ants.

A vast column of army ants marches across a rainforest floor in South America. The ants work together to outnumber and overwhelm their prey, which may include cockroaches, scorpions, crickets, and small lizards. Using their stings and strong jaws, an army ant swarm may make thousands of kills every day.

Robber flies hover, hoping to pick off insects escaping from the ants.

HELPING EACH OTHER

When species help each other, both may benefit from the relationship such as when a bee feeds on nectar from a flower and, in return, disperses the flower's pollen. This rhino has iticks removed from its body by oxpecker birds which, in return, get an easy meal.

Oxpeckers may signal alarm if a predator approaches, warning the rhino.

Ants release a chemical trail for other members of the colony to follow.

TAKEOFF

Most bats cannot take off from the ground because their wings do not provide enough lift, nor can they run forward fast enough to take off. Instead, they use the height of their roost to launch themselves into the air.

Wing membrane is very light, making bats more agile in flight than birds.

Bats do not flap forelimbs, as birds do, but flap their spread-out digits.

Chest and shoulders have strong muscles to help move wings.

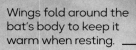

Wings fold around the bat's body to keep it warm when resting.

HOW DO BATS SLEEP?

Most bats are nocturnal, meaning that they are active at night and rest during the day. Bats are unusual because they sleep upside down, hanging from a tree branch, cave roof, or even the undersides of bridges and tunnels.

Bats sleep in this way for several reasons. It enables them to rest in places that are difficult for daytime predators to spot or reach. It also gives them some height above ground, which helps when they wish to take off (see above). To hang and rest, a bat flies into position, opens the claws on its toes and grips the surface. By letting its body's muscles relax, the weight of the bat hanging down causes its claws to close, locking it into position to rest.

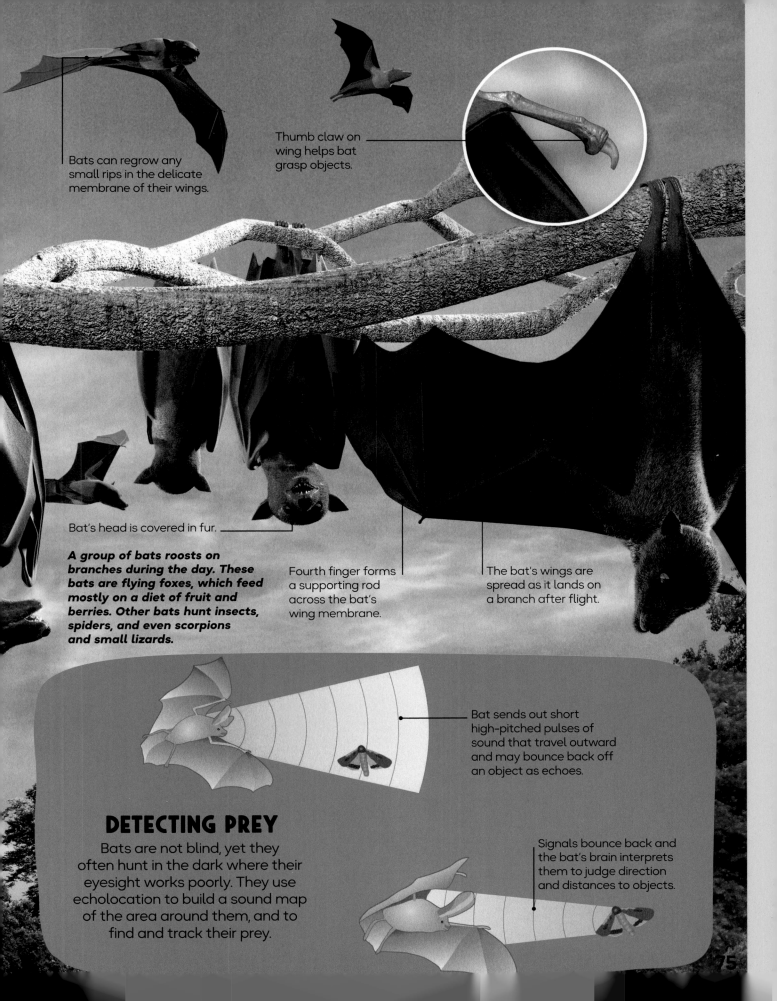

Bats can regrow any small rips in the delicate membrane of their wings.

Thumb claw on wing helps bat grasp objects.

Bat's head is covered in fur.

A group of bats roosts on branches during the day. These bats are flying foxes, which feed mostly on a diet of fruit and berries. Other bats hunt insects, spiders, and even scorpions and small lizards.

Fourth finger forms a supporting rod across the bat's wing membrane.

The bat's wings are spread as it lands on a branch after flight.

Bat sends out short high-pitched pulses of sound that travel outward and may bounce back off an object as echoes.

DETECTING PREY

Bats are not blind, yet they often hunt in the dark where their eyesight works poorly. They use echolocation to build a sound map of the area around them, and to find and track their prey.

Signals bounce back and the bat's brain interprets them to judge direction and distances to objects.

HOW DO CREATURES BREATHE UNDERWATER?

Thousands of different species live in water but still require oxygen for their bodies to respire and produce energy. These creatures obtain oxygen either by surfacing to breathe in air or by extracting oxygen from the water around them.

There are more than 34,000 species of fish, almost all of which do not possess lungs. Instead, they channel water over organs called gills, which draw in oxygen from the water. Other creatures, besides fish, have gills. These include mollusks such as mussels, octopuses, and clams. Crabs and other crustaceans, such as shrimps, also possess gills, but some underwater life—bacteria, for example—can absorb oxygen from water through their outer membranes. Marine mammals such as seals, dolphins, and whales all possess lungs like land animals do and need to surface regularly to breathe. Some whales can stay underwater for an hour or longer between breaths.

Large gill slits on the underside of the manta ray.

Body can measure 98 ft. (30m) in length and weigh more than 187 tons.

Blue whales have two blowholes that can take in up to 1,320 gal. (5,000L) of air into their lungs.

An average adult manta ray is about 21 ft. (6.5m) wide and can weigh 1.4 tons (1,300kg).

COMING UP FOR AIR

Cetaceans are a family of mammals that includes whales, dolphins, and porpoise. They have nostrils, or blowholes, on top of their heads, which close up when they dive, but open when the creatures surface to breathe in air.

Manta rays are large fish with winglike pectoral fins that glide gracefully through the water. They feed on about 44 to 66 lb. (20 to 30kg) of plankton and fish larvae each day. Like all fish, they obtain oxygen from the sea water using their gills.

GILLS

A fish draws water across its gills. Oxygen diffuses out of the water and into the gill's blood vessels. At the same time, carbon dioxide leaves the blood vessels and exits from the gills.

1. Water is drawn through the fish's mouth, and comblike gill rakers filter out any food particles from the water.

Gills

Gill rakers trap particles.

Gill filaments

2. As the water moves across the gills, some of the oxygen it contains dissolves in the tiny blood vessels found in the gill filaments.

Oxygen-rich blood flows away from gills.

Flow of water

3. Carbon dioxide leaves the blood and enters the water. The operculum, a bony flap that covers the gills, opens to let the water flow out of the fish.

Oxygen-poor blood flows to gills.

Pectoral fins can flap like wings, helping the fish move through water.

Short, narrow tail contains no bones or stinging cells.

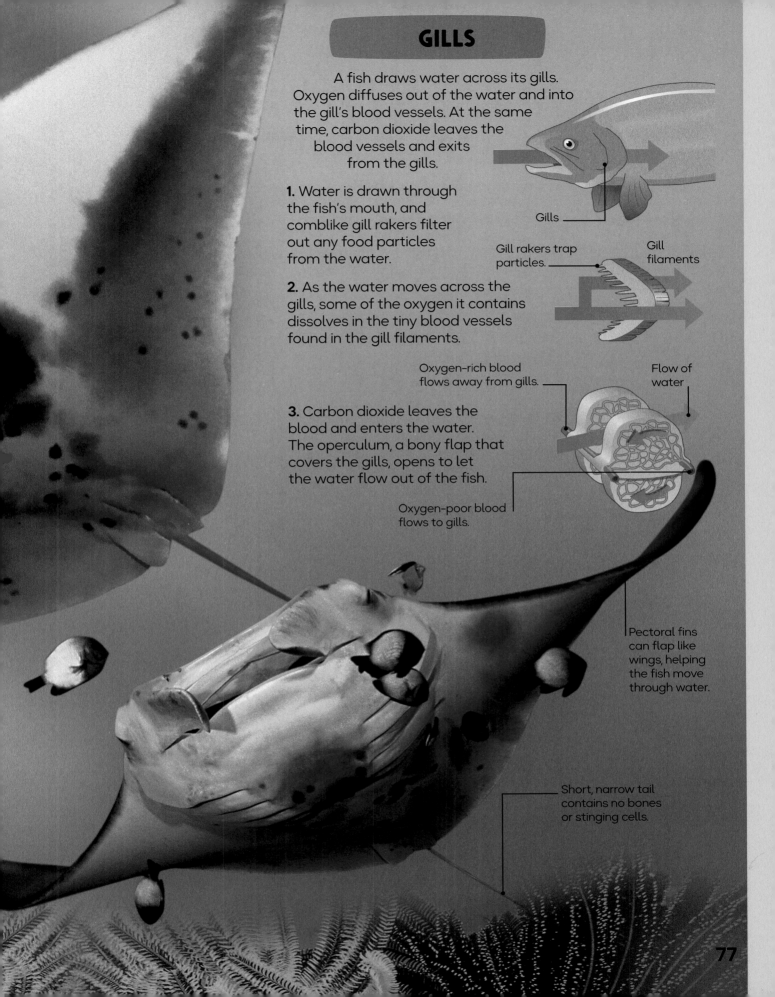

FLEXIBLE BONES

Cheetahs have very flexible backbones that bend like a spring with every stride taken. This adds power to each step the creature takes.

Long tail helps balance the cheetah when it runs and turns at high speed.

Long, thin leg bones to which powerful muscles are attached.

Large rib cage to house enlarged heart and lungs.

Dorsal fin grows to 3 ft. (1m) high, then retracts when the fish swims at maximum speed, to cut down drag.

Slender, streamlined body helps cut through water fast.

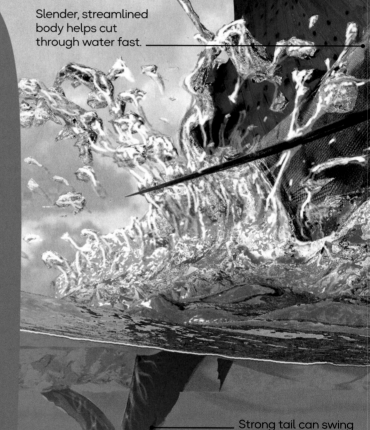

ACCELERATION

A cheetah can accelerate from a standstill to more than 37 mph (60km/h) in just three strides by using its powerful muscles and flexible skeleton. It can reach 62 mph (100km/h) in only three seconds.

1. Cheetah strides forward, pushing off its hard footpads and dropping its head slightly.

2. Spine bends and coils up like a spring as the rear legs travel forward.

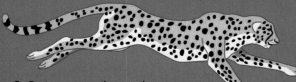

3. Spine uncoils at the same time as leg muscles push the cheetah forward with great power, taking a 24-ft. (7.5-m) -long bound.

Strong tail can swing back and forth to generate the great power needed to swim quickly.

Upper jaw forms long, swordlike bill, at least twice the length of lower jaw.

A sailfish leaps out of the water. This large ocean fish can swim at speeds of 37 to 40 mph (60 to 65km/h) for long periods of time. When chasing prey or evading capture, its powerful body and tail can propel it to speeds of 68 mph (110km/h).

HOW DO THE FASTEST CREATURES ACCELERATE?

The fastest creatures on land, as well as in the air and sea, use their great speed to catch other fast-moving prey. They are all streamlined so that they can move through air or water with as little resistance as possible.

Pointed mouth catches fish and crustaceans.

Sailfish can grow to 8 to 10 ft. (2.5 to 3.1m) long and weigh 200 lb. (90kg).

Each record-breaking creature has adaptations to their body that help them move as rapidly and as efficiently as possible. The cheetah, for example, is lightweight—usually weighing less than 130 lb. (60kg)—and has a larger heart and lungs than other mammals of a similar size. These help to supply its body with enough oxygen during its high-speed sprints of up to 75 mph (120km/h). Both the sailfish (the fastest fish) and the peregrine falcon (the fastest bird) can pull in body parts to create as smooth, sleek, and fast a shape as possible and have powerful muscles to drive them forward.

FASTEST BIRD

Peregrine falcons fly to high altitudes and dive steeply in order to catch their prey. As they dive, their pointed wings are tucked in tightly to create a shape that cuts through the air easily. They can reach speeds of up to 200 mph (320km/h), faster than any other bird. .

Slim, stiff feathers

Pointed wings tucked in during dive for high speed.

HOW DO ANIMALS MIGRATE?

Many living things go on long migration journeys at the same time every year. They go in search of food, water, a place to breed, or, as the seasons change, an environment with a more suitable climate.

Often, migrating animals travel in large numbers—in herds, flocks, or schools that offer them protection and help in finding the way. Some species may use familiar geographical landmarks and certain smells and tastes as a guide. Others may be able to sense changes in Earth's magnetic field, giving them an internal compass that helps them find north or south. Animals also have to know when to migrate and often use changes in temperature or "photoperiod"—the amount of daylight in a day—as a guide. Shorter days tell them that the winter is approaching.

Every year, a great herd of wildebeests travels up to 1,550 mi. (2,500km) across Africa's Serengeti Plain. The animals go in search of the lush, mineral-rich grasslands that help keep them healthy. Herds can include hundreds of thousands of individuals.

Wildebeests follow the herd up a steep bank on their way to food-rich grasslands.

MONARCH BUTTERLY

These butterflies cannot survive the winters of Canada and the northern United States. At the end of every summer, they fly south, traveling up to 2,730 mi. (4,400km) to spend the winter in Mexico or California.

Antenna helps the butterfly navigate, using the Sun as a guide.

Each front hoof of a wildebeest leaves a trail of scent for other wildebeests to follow.

Butterfly's abdomen contains its heart and most of its digestive system.

Wingspan measures 4 in. (10cm) at its widest point.

Arctic

Migration route northward

Migration routes southward

Atlantic Ocean

Africa

South America

Antarctica

Southern Ocean

ARCTIC TERN

Every August or September, arctic terns make an astonishing, long-range migration from deep inside the Arctic Circle to Antarctica, flying down the African or South American coastline. They return to the Arctic the following spring.

Arctic tern's wingspan is 30 to 34 in. (76 to 85cm), yet the bird is light, weighing as little as 3.5 oz. (100g).

CARIBOU HERDS

Each year, herds of caribou migrate to the open Arctic tundra in the summer, where they eat up to 11 lb. (5kg) of plants a day. In the winter, herds move to forest regions, sometimes swimming across lakes and sea bays along the way.

Clouds of dust billow up from the trampling of the ground by all the wildebeests' hooves.

1. One or more chimps act as "drivers," climbing up the tree beneath their prey. The driver chimps start chasing the monkeys through the tree canopy.

2. As the colobus monkeys flee from the drivers, blockers run forward, anticipating where their prey will head. The blockers climb trees, then reveal themselves to the monkeys, screaming and waving their arms.

3. The terrified monkeys are driven between the blockers. Ahead hides an ambusher—the most experienced hunter in the group of chimps—who lies in wait for the fleeing monkeys.

4. The ambusher attacks. If a colobus spots the ambusher and tries to retreat, it will probably fall prey to one of the other chimps in the hunting party.

Blocker cuts off escape route.

Driver

Blocker

Driver

Chimps usually hunt in the dry season, when there are fewer fruit and nuts to eat.

Colobus monkey

Ambusher shows himself at the last minute.

HOW DO CHIMPS HUNT?

Chimpanzees in West Africa eat fruit, nuts, and leaves, but sometimes go hunting. Red colobus monkeys, which are light, agile and good at leaping from tree to tree, are the chimpanzees' main prey. Chimps are heavy, with some weighing nearly as much as a man. On its own, a chimp could not catch a colobus. But by working together in cunning ways, chimps can herd colobus monkeys into a trap.

HOW DO CARNIVOROUS PLANTS TRAP PREY?

Carnivorous (meat-eating) plants trap and digest flies, insects, and spiders. The Venus flytrap grows in bogs where the acidic soil lacks certain nutrients the plant needs. So it lures insects to its leaves by producing sweet, sticky nectar, then digests them gain the missing nutrients.

This Venus fly trap is one of more than 500 types of carnivorous plants.

1. Each pair of leaves has three "trigger" hairs. If an insect walks over two triggers in a 20- to 30-second period, the fly trap springs into action.

2. The leaves snap shut in half a second. Finger-like prongs called cilia, around the edge of each leaf, keep larger insects inside. Smaller insects, not worth digesting, are able to escape.

3. The leaves close fully, trapping the insect. The plant pumps out digestive juices that dissolve the soft, inner parts of the insect but leave any hard, bony parts.

4. Digestion takes 5 to 12 days. Then the leaves open, the leftover body parts are blown away or washed away by rain, and the plant is ready for its next victim.

SUPERFAST SNAP

Bladderworts are underwater carnivorous plants. Some species have the fastest traps of all, taking just 1/30th of a second to capture prey—many times faster than a Venus flytrap.

Long cilia lock together to trap prey.

HOW DO SHARKS SENSE PREY?

Sharks are among the natural world's most accomplished predators, able to detect and hunt down prey from long distances away. Key to their success is the large range of sophisticated and accurate senses they possess.

Sharks have large eyes that give them keen eyesight in gloomy, deep water where there's little light. A shark uses its hearing to pick up low-frequency sounds. It also has an exceptionally strong sense of smell (see right), and can even detect tiny electrical signals given off by other sea creatures' hearts and muscles. This enables sharks to seek out prey that may be hiding in sand on the ocean floor. Once the prey is located, sharks move quickly and attack with powerful jaws filled with large, sharp teeth.

Large stomach secretes powerful acids to digest any prey caught and eaten.

Powerful tail muscles and fin help propel the shark through water at speeds of up to 15 mph (24km/h).

Pectoral fins are used to lift and steer the body as it travels forward.

Torpedo-shaped body is streamlined to travel quickly and easily through water.

SENSE RANGES

A shark's senses work at different distances. For example, sharks sense water temperature and touch only through their skin, but they can detect sounds over many miles.

Vision up to 164 ft. (50m)

Smell (used from 328 ft./ 100m up to several miles)

Electrical signals up to 20 in. (50cm)

Vibrations sensed as changes in water pressure (up to 328 ft./100m)

Hearing (used over distances of more than 0.6 mi./1km)

0	3 ft. (1m)	33 ft. (10m)	328 ft. (100m)	3,280 ft. (1,000m)	6.2 mi. (10,000m)

A great white shark swoops to catch a seal in its giant, teeth-lined jaws. These fearsome predatory fish, one of more than 400 species of sharks, can grow to between 15 and 21 ft. (4.6 and 6.4m) long and weigh as much as 6,600 lb. (3,000kg).

Shark's snout is flexible and cushioned for impact with the body of its prey.

SHARK'S HEAD

As fish, sharks have gills that obtain oxygen from water. They have nostrils, but use them for smell and not for breathing. Some sharks can smell a small amount of blood in the water from more than 1 mi. (1,500m) away.

Nostrils channel water into nasal cavities where sense organs detect smells.

Forward-facing eyes can judge distances to objects accurately.

Lower jaw is hinged and opens widely to catch large prey.

Mouth filled with as many as 300 triangular-shaped teeth in rows.

Lateral line

LATERAL LINE

A long row of tiny, fluid-filled vessels called neuromasts run the length of a shark's body. These help it sense vibrations in water caused by the movement of injured fish or marine mammals thrashing around.

A diamondback rattlesnake, so named for its distinctive body markings, closes in on a collared lizard, ready for the kill. The snake will strike with its large, curved fangs and inject venom into the lizard. This type of snake also preys upon small mammals.

Rattle on the end of its tail may warn predators or hoofed animals away from the snake.

Long, flexible body may grow up to 6.6 to 8.2 ft. (2 to 2.5m) in length.

HOW DO SNAKES KILL?

Snakes are carnivores equipped with a large range of senses used for hunting, and often ambushing, their prey. While their eyesight is not well developed, their senses of hearing, touch, and especially taste and smell, are strong.

A snake flicks its tongue to collect airborne particles that it then wipes on the roof of its mouth. There, a special organ called the vomeronasal organ (or Jacobson's organ) helps the brain identify smells. Rattlesnakes have highly sensitive heat-sensing organs between their eyes and nose that can track prey in complete darkness. Many snakes are venomous, using fangs to inject poison into their prey. Others capture and swallow prey whole or may first wrap their body tightly around it and squeeze it to death. Some snakes have unusual killing methods. The Australian Woma python, for example, pushes and crushes small rodents against the wall of its prey's burrow.

SWALLOWING WHOLE

A snake cannot chew its prey, so it must swallow it whole. Very flexible jaws allow it to swallow prey much larger than itself. The snake becomes dormant while it digests, but may regurgitate (throw up) the prey if it needs to escape danger.

VENOMOUS SNAKES

A snake's venom is produced and stored in a pair of venom glands, one under each eye. Venom varies in strength between different snakes, but it contains toxins that damage the prey's heart and blood vessels and may cause its breathing to stop.

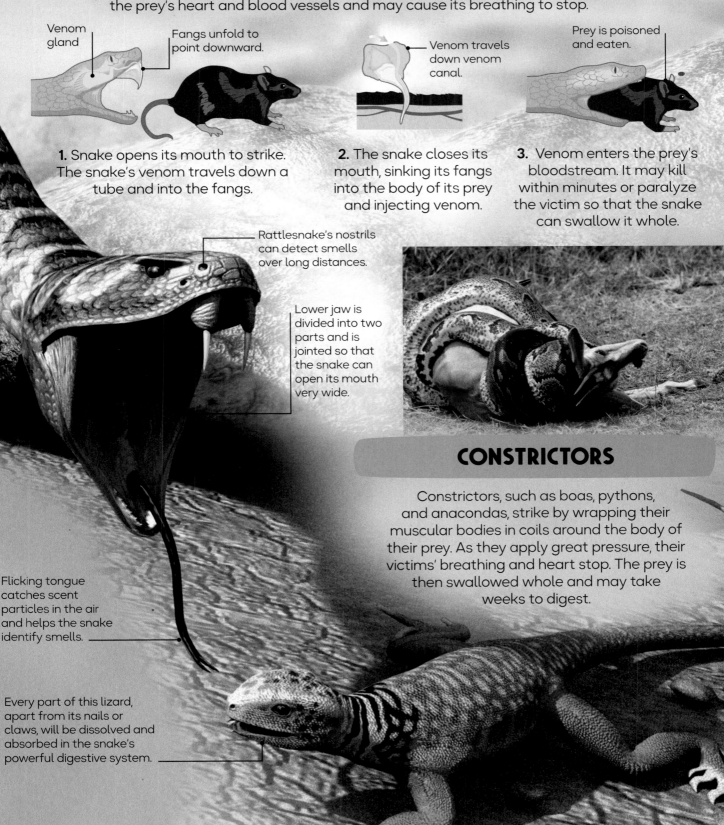

Venom gland

Fangs unfold to point downward.

Venom travels down venom canal.

Prey is poisoned and eaten.

1. Snake opens its mouth to strike. The snake's venom travels down a tube and into the fangs.

2. The snake closes its mouth, sinking its fangs into the body of its prey and injecting venom.

3. Venom enters the prey's bloodstream. It may kill within minutes or paralyze the victim so that the snake can swallow it whole.

Rattlesnake's nostrils can detect smells over long distances.

Lower jaw is divided into two parts and is jointed so that the snake can open its mouth very wide.

Flicking tongue catches scent particles in the air and helps the snake identify smells.

Every part of this lizard, apart from its nails or claws, will be dissolved and absorbed in the snake's powerful digestive system.

CONSTRICTORS

Constrictors, such as boas, pythons, and anacondas, strike by wrapping their muscular bodies in coils around the body of their prey. As they apply great pressure, their victims' breathing and heart stop. The prey is then swallowed whole and may take weeks to digest.

HOW DO SPECIES BECOME ENDANGERED?

All around the world, hundreds of different living things—from plants and insects to birds, fish, and large mammals—are endangered. This means that an entire species may become extinct (die out). There are many reasons why this can occur.

Throughout Earth's natural history, species of living things have flourished and then become extinct. In recent centuries, however, the increasing impact of human activity on the environment has meant that many successful species are faced with the threat of extinction. Pollution from industrial processes and accidents such as chemical and oil spills have damaged environments and threatened certain species. Other threatening activities include overfishing and hunting animals for food and fur, or, in the case of rhinos, for their horns. One of the most common threats in some parts of the world is habitat destruction. This is where the natural homes and environments of living things are destroyed—by draining wetlands or cutting down forests, for example.

Here, a polar bear hunts a beluga whale. Polar bears in some areas of the Arctic are endangered because of pollution and climate change, which is melting the Arctic sea ice where many polar bears live.

Rear legs are used in water as a rudder for steering.

In the water, polar bears normally swim using their front legs.

Polar bears are able to dive to depths of up to 15 ft. (4.5m) and stay underwater for more than a minute.

JAGUAR

The jaguar has almost completely disappeared from the United States and is endangered elsewhere. This is because people hunt it for its beautiful fur coat, and because its forest habitats are being destroyed.

Powerful jaws used to kill prey with one crushing bite.

Front paws contain retractable claws that spring out when hunting.

Fur covers a thick layer of blubber that insulates the polar bear and keeps it warm.

Large parts of the Borneo Rainforest are undisturbed and unexplored.

Trees are cleared as farming, industry, and human settlements spread.

Borneo Island

1950

Borneo Island

2020

SHRINKING FORESTS

The scale of habitat destruction becomes clear when we look at how dramatically the world's forests have shrunk over the past 10,000 years as the human population has grown. The Borneo Rainforest (above) has shrunk rapidly in just 70 years, as trees have been cleared for farmland or new settlements or for timber or firewood.

Short, curved claws can dig into and grip prey.

CANE TOADS

Species introduced by humans to new regions can sometimes spread and destroy populations of other living things. A handful of cane toads were introduced into Australia in the 1930s. They now number many millions, compete for food with other species, and kill frogs, quolls, and other creatures with their poisonous skin.

Jaws and teeth are used to bite and kill seals, walrus, and small whales.

HOW DO OXYGEN AND NUTRIENTS TRAVEL?

Humans need oxygen to be constantly carried around their bodies. Cells use this oxygen to release energy from sugars during the process of respiration. They also need nutrients to be transported through their bodies. Both tasks are performed by the blood in the circulatory system.

The human body contains about 1.3 gal. (5L) of blood, which is constantly circulated throughout the body by the heart—a large, muscular pump with four chambers. This pumps (beats) about 70 times every minute, effectively moving approximately 1,980 gal. (7,500L) of blood around the body every day. The blood travels inside a vast network of blood vessels to all parts of the body, delivering oxygen to cells and carrying away waste carbon dioxide. Nutrients from digested food are mostly absorbed into blood from the small intestine so that they can then be carried throughout the body as well.

Here, a blood vessel is cut away to reveal the blood cells traveling through it. More than half of blood is made up of plasma—a thin, watery substance that carries absorbed nutrients and vitamins around the body.

Right atrium

Oxygen-rich blood leaves the heart via the aorta—the largest blood vessel in the body.

Pulmonary artery carries blood from heart to lungs.

Pulmonary veins carry blood from lungs back to the heart.

Left atrium

Right ventricle

Left ventricle

Oxygen binds with a substance called hemoglobin in red blood cells. This gives blood its color.

BEATING HEART

Blood low in oxygen enters the first heart chamber— the right atrium. From there, it is pumped through the right ventricle up and out of the heart to the lungs, where it obtains more oxygen. The blood returns to the left atrium and travels to the left ventricle, from where it is pumped out and around the body.

White blood cell helps fight infections and germs.

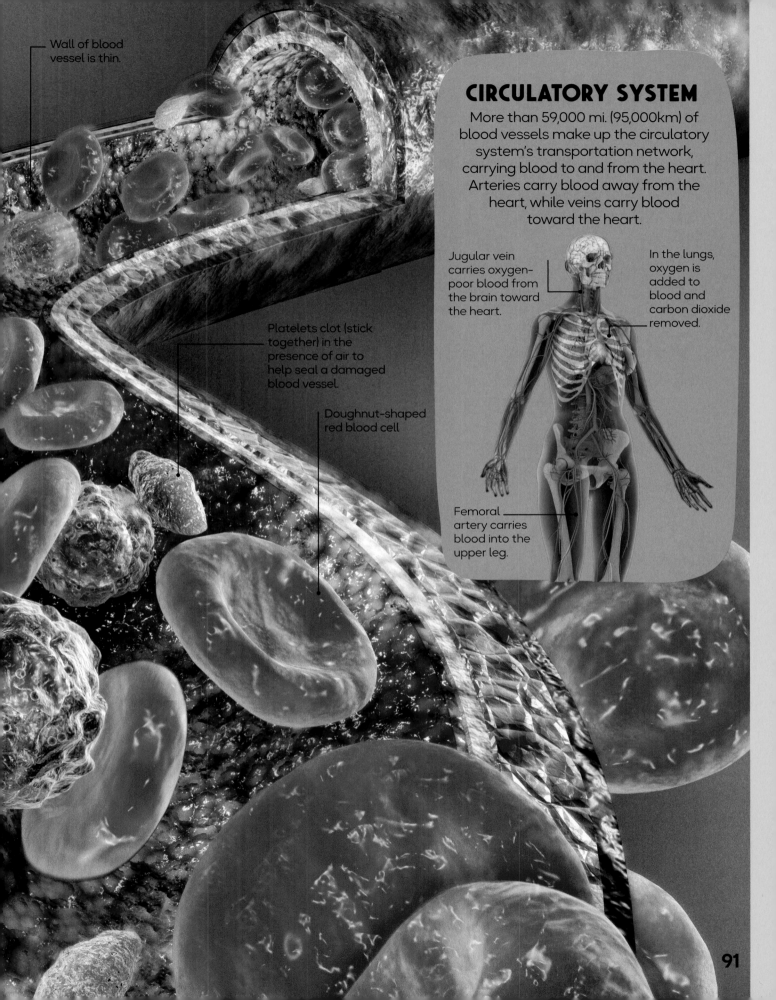

Wall of blood vessel is thin.

Platelets clot (stick together) in the presence of air to help seal a damaged blood vessel.

Doughnut-shaped red blood cell

CIRCULATORY SYSTEM

More than 59,000 mi. (95,000km) of blood vessels make up the circulatory system's transportation network, carrying blood to and from the heart. Arteries carry blood away from the heart, while veins carry blood toward the heart.

Jugular vein carries oxygen-poor blood from the brain toward the heart.

In the lungs, oxygen is added to blood and carbon dioxide removed.

Femoral artery carries blood into the upper leg.

HOW DO HUMANS RUN?

Running fast requires a number of the human body's major systems to work well together. These include the muscular system as well as the skeleton and its joints, which provide the moving framework that supports the rest of the body.

More than 600 skeletal muscles are attached to bones via tendons. These muscles contract (get shorter) or relax to provide the force that moves the body's parts. Running involves many more muscles than just those that lift and drive the legs forward to take long, quick strides. The arms must pump back and forth, while the muscles in the core of the body must be strong to maintain a balanced posture. Working your muscles hard to run at high speed makes great demands on other parts of your body. The rate of breathing increases to draw in more oxygen, and the heart beats faster to pump blood around the body more quickly, so that oxygen and nutrients can reach the muscles.

An athlete starts a race, pushing his legs out of the starting blocks in order to sprint down a track. Many muscles in his body must work together efficiently for him to run smoothly and quickly.

Gluteus maximus muscle is the largest individual muscle in the human body. It helps maintain the body's posture.

Hamstring muscle bends leg at the knee.

MUSCLE CONTRACTION

Each skeletal muscle is made of large bundles of long cells called fibers. Nerve signals travel from the brain to the muscles, causing the muscle fibers to contract and pull the bones to which they are attached.

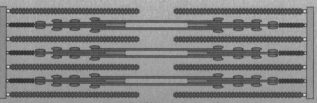

Muscle fiber relaxes

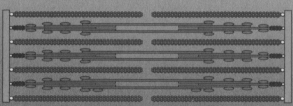

Muscle fiber contracts

Rear foot drives hard out of the starting block as the leg straightens.

Gastrocnemius muscle bends foot downward and also flexes the knee.

Deltoid muscle helps move arm backward and then forward during run.

Head kept down in first few paces of sprint but will lift as the body rises.

Biceps relax as triceps contract to pull arm downward.

Biceps contract to pull lower arm up.

Triceps relax

Biceps muscle helps bend arm at the elbow.

Front leg drives up and forward to take the first stride in the run.

Runner will land on the ball of his foot.

ANTAGONISTIC PAIRS

A single muscle can pull parts of the body only in one direction. So muscles are grouped around the body in antagonistic pairs, such as the biceps and triceps muscles in your upper arm. Together, they can move the arm in different directions.

THE WORLD'S FASTEST HUMAN

Usain Bolt of Jamaica crosses the finish line to win a men's sprint race. In 2009, Bolt ran the world's fastest-ever 100m time of 9.58 seconds, averaging a speed throughout the race of 23.35 mph (37.58km/h).

HOW DO OPTICAL ILLUSIONS FOOL THE BRAIN?

Optical illusions use color, light, and patterns to create images that trick your brain into seeing something that is not there or mislead it in some other way. This happens for a range of reasons.

For a strong sense of vision, your brain must process millions of signals from your eyes continuously. It must make sense of the signals using experience and knowledge, looking for patterns and recognizable objects. Sometimes it fills in gaps to see objects it is familiar with, or groups random objects together in patterns it understands. Optical illusions make use of the way the brain makes assumptions. They trick it into filling in a shape or misjudging the sizes of two same-size objects.

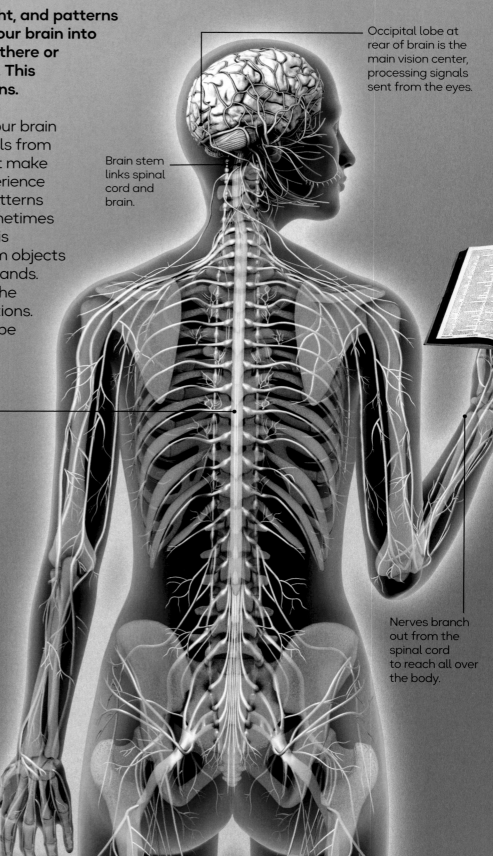

Occipital lobe at rear of brain is the main vision center, processing signals sent from the eyes.

Brain stem links spinal cord and brain.

Spinal cord carries large numbers of signals from all parts of the body to the brain.

Nerves branch out from the spinal cord to reach all over the body.

NERVOUS SYSTEM

A vast network of nerve fibers, each made up of neurons (nerve cells), runs through the human body carrying signals. Sensory nerves carry signals to the brain from parts of the body, while motor nerves carry instructions from the brain to move muscles, for example.

WHICH IS LONGER?

The bottom horizontal line appears shorter, but it is an optical illusion. Both lines are the same length. Your brain is tricked by the different angle of the arrowheads to believe that the top horizontal line is longer.

To read words on the page or view pictures, the eye must focus on the page and send signals captured by its retina (see below) along the optic nerve to the brain.

Skull, made up of bony plates, protects the delicate brain inside.

Lacrimal gland secretes tears that keep the front of the eye moist and wash away dust and dirt.

The eye's curved lens is protected by a transparent cover called the cornea.

Image signals collected by retina at back of eye.

Pupil adjusts amount of light let into the eye.

The eye is held in its skull socket by a series of muscles called the muscles of orbit. They control the movement of the eye.

Lens focuses image, which travels through the pupil into the eye.

INSIDE THE EYE

Light passes through the clear lens of the eye, which focuses it on the rear of the eye—the retina. There, light-sensitive rod and cone cells convert the image into electrical signals sent to the brain via the optic nerve.

LIFE
FIND OUT MORE ABOUT HOW THE WORLD WORKS

WEBSITES TO VISIT

www.nhm.ac.uk/discover/mammals.html
Learn more about all kinds of animals from the website of the Natural History Museum, London, U.K.

https://askabiologist.asu.edu/images/zoom/ant-gallery-get-close-ants
A fascinating gallery of photos from Arizona State University shows how ants live and work in colonies.

www.bats.org.uk
Find out lots more about bats and how they live at the web pages of the U.K. Bat Conservation Trust.

www.sharktrust.org
Learn the facts about one of the most misunderstood groups of creatures on the planet—sharks. This web site includes a database of shark species and facts about shark biology.

www.cheetah.org
The Cheetah Conservation Fund web site contains images and facts about the world's fastest land mammal.

www.activewild.com/endangered-animals-facts-for-kids/
Pick up valuable and accurate information on many different endangered species.

www.bhf.org.uk/heart-health/how-your-heart-works.aspx
See how a healthy heart works at these web pages brought to you by the British Heart Foundation.

http://faculty.washington.edu/chudler/introb.html
Explore the brain and nervous system and learn about brain development, the nervous system, nerve disorders, and much, much more at this web site hosted by neuroscientist Dr. Eric H. Chudler.

http://science.howstuffworks.com/life/human-biology/eye1.htm
Learn more about how the human eye works and enables us to see.

www.kids.niehs.nih.gov/games/riddles/illusions/index.htm
Enjoy this large collection of optical illusions at the National Institute of Environmental Health Sciences' web pages for children.

CHAPTER FOUR

SCIENCE AND TECHNOLOGY

HOW ARE VIDEO GAMES CREATED?

Many video games are the work of large teams. A game starts out as a story idea that is then storyboarded (sketched out) by game designers to portray all the different scenes and options that can occur.

The storyboard gives a visual plot of the game and how it can be played. It must allow for every outcome that a player may choose during the game. A large team of artists and animators design all the game's scenes, objects, and characters. Others work on the music and sound effects, while voice actors record the game dialogue. As all the different parts come together, the game is tested rigorously for any bugs (flaws or errors). Sometimes, an early version of the game is released to experienced gamers so they can test it fully and identify any problems.

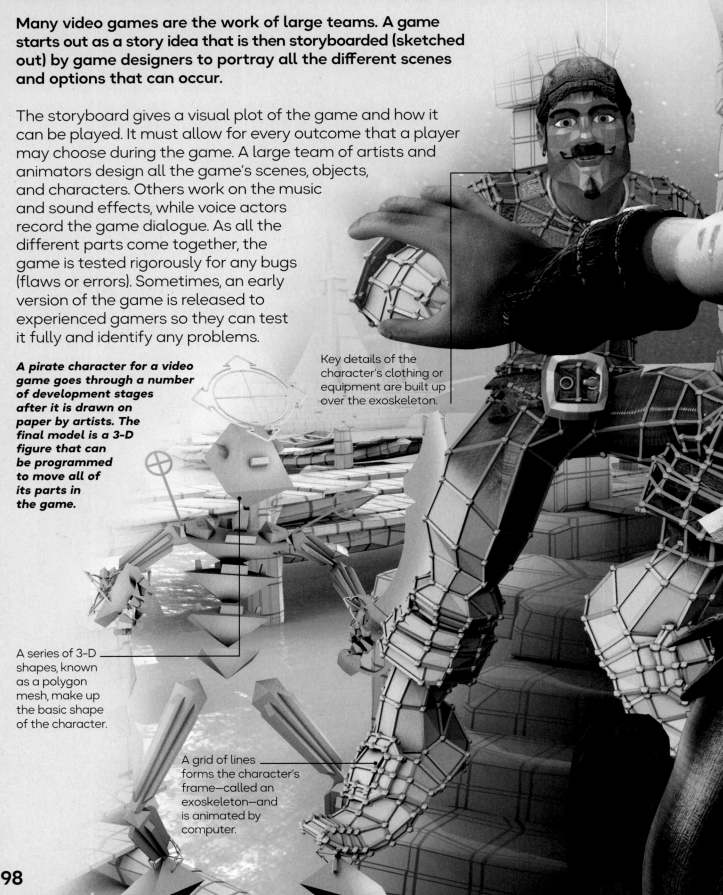

A pirate character for a video game goes through a number of development stages after it is drawn on paper by artists. The final model is a 3-D figure that can be programmed to move all of its parts in the game.

Key details of the character's clothing or equipment are built up over the exoskeleton.

A series of 3-D shapes, known as a polygon mesh, make up the basic shape of the character.

A grid of lines forms the character's frame—called an exoskeleton—and is animated by computer.

Character's skin and clothing are rendered (finished in detail) by computers to give a polished 3-D appearance.

GAME PROGRAMMING

Behind the scenes and action in a game lie thousands, sometimes millions, of lines of code that generate the environment, the game's rules, and the ways by which characters and objects move. Teams of programmers are responsible for getting all of this code correct and fully working.

MOTION CAPTURE

National Basketball Association (NBA) star Tony Parker wears a motion-control suit. Game designers are using data from the suit to capture Parker's movements accurately on a computer for use in a basketball game.

Sensors called trackers record body movements.

HOW DO ROBOTS FIND THEIR WAY?

Mobile robots can move from place to place on land, in the air, in space, or underwater. Many are remote-controlled from a distance by a human operator, but some robots navigate themselves to their target.

A robot has a range of devices called sensors. These gather information about the robot itself and the area around it and send the data to the robot's controller, usually an onboard computer. The controller makes decisions based on the data and instructs all the parts of the robot. Some mobile robots are equipped with many different sensors that build up a detailed data picture of their environment. This information may be used with a global positioning system (GPS) to plot the robot's route, while proximity sensors measure the distances to obstacles and objects.

Two different mobile robots attend to an injured soldier. The larger is a Battlefield Extraction-Assist Robot (BEAR). In the future, robots like these may work by themselves, finding wounded soldiers or injured people to lift and rescue in disaster areas.

Sensors inside track units tell the robot's controller the speed and angle at which they're moving.

Tracks allow the robot to climb over obstacles and travel across rough ground.

Laser rangefinder sensor helps the robot's controller judge the distances to objects ahead.

UNDERWATER ROBOTS

Some robots can navigate underwater for voyages lasting many days or weeks at a time. Many use sonar, which bounces high-pitch sound signals off nearby objects to determine the objects' distance from the robot.

Hydraulic-powered arms can lift more than 440 lb. (200kg). They slide under the figure on the ground and lift him up.

Cameras in the robot's head process views of the terrain.

Tail helps keep the drone stable when in the air.

Nose camera

DRONES

Unmanned aircrafts, or drones, first appeared in the 1990s. They are now used for all kinds of purposes, from military surveillance and strikes against enemy targets, to filming, delivering goods, monitoring conservation, and leisure.

In the future, soldiers may carry a tracking sensor that will allow a robot to locate their position and come to their aid.

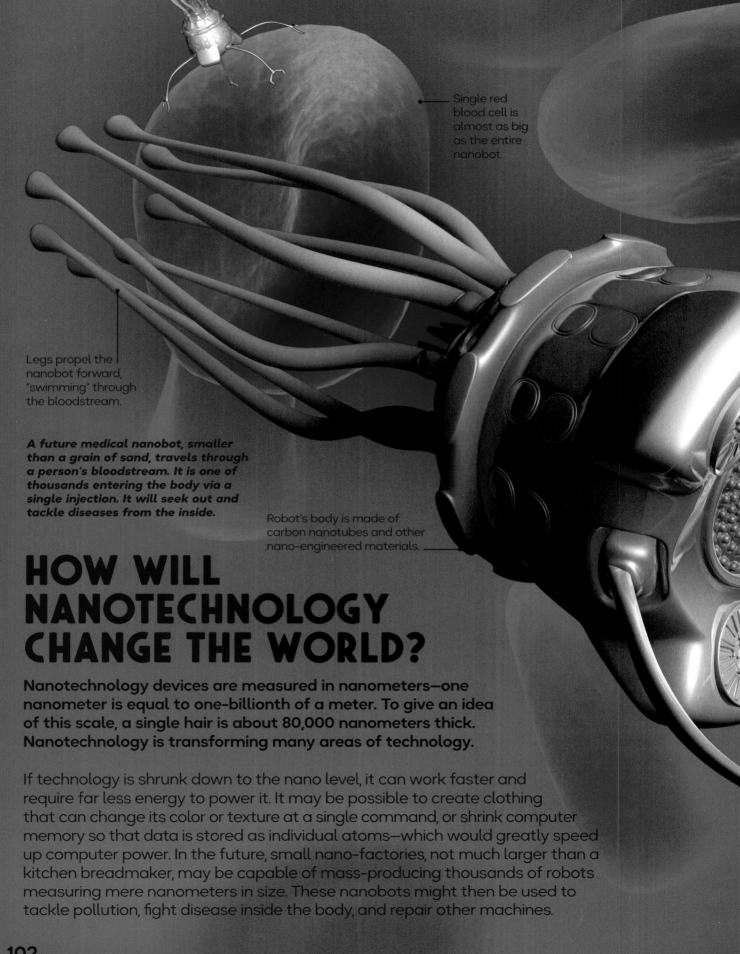

Single red blood cell is almost as big as the entire nanobot.

Legs propel the nanobot forward, "swimming" through the bloodstream.

A future medical nanobot, smaller than a grain of sand, travels through a person's bloodstream. It is one of thousands entering the body via a single injection. It will seek out and tackle diseases from the inside.

Robot's body is made of carbon nanotubes and other nano-engineered materials.

HOW WILL NANOTECHNOLOGY CHANGE THE WORLD?

Nanotechnology devices are measured in nanometers—one nanometer is equal to one-billionth of a meter. To give an idea of this scale, a single hair is about 80,000 nanometers thick. Nanotechnology is transforming many areas of technology.

If technology is shrunk down to the nano level, it can work faster and require far less energy to power it. It may be possible to create clothing that can change its color or texture at a single command, or shrink computer memory so that data is stored as individual atoms—which would greatly speed up computer power. In the future, small nano-factories, not much larger than a kitchen breadmaker, may be capable of mass-producing thousands of robots measuring mere nanometers in size. These nanobots might then be used to tackle pollution, fight disease inside the body, and repair other machines.

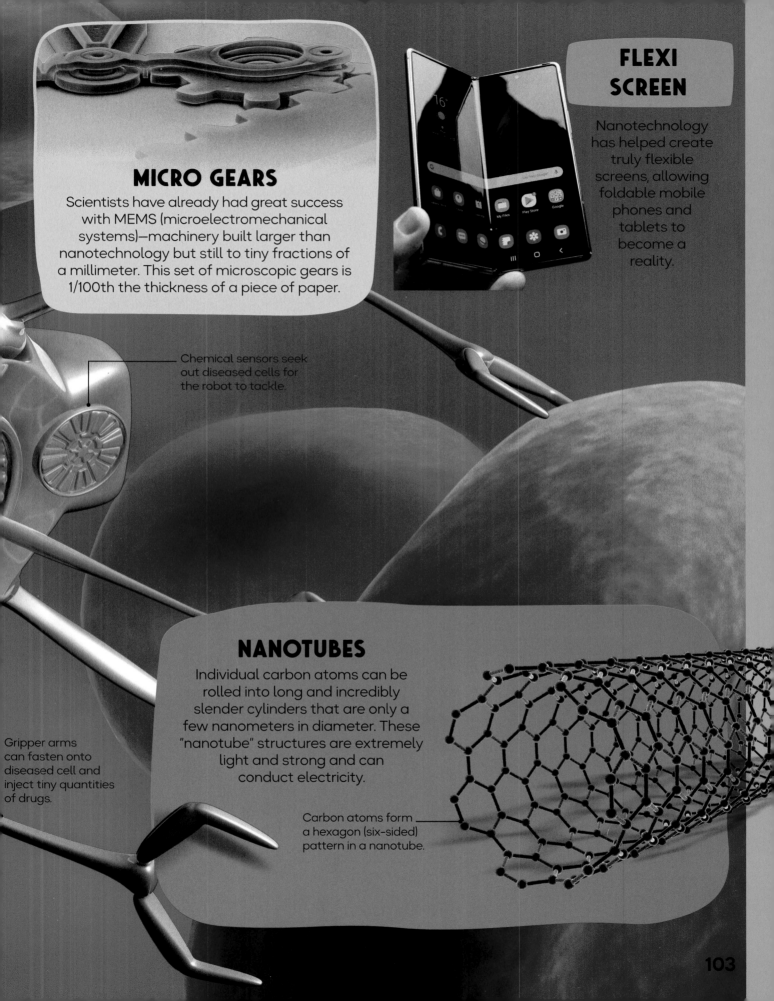

MICRO GEARS

Scientists have already had great success with MEMS (microelectromechanical systems)—machinery built larger than nanotechnology but still to tiny fractions of a millimeter. This set of microscopic gears is 1/100th the thickness of a piece of paper.

Nanotechnology has helped create truly flexible screens, allowing foldable mobile phones and tablets to become a reality.

Chemical sensors seek out diseased cells for the robot to tackle.

Gripper arms can fasten onto diseased cell and inject tiny quantities of drugs.

NANOTUBES

Individual carbon atoms can be rolled into long and incredibly slender cylinders that are only a few nanometers in diameter. These "nanotube" structures are extremely light and strong and can conduct electricity.

Carbon atoms form a hexagon (six-sided) pattern in a nanotube.

FUEL RODS

The reactor's energy is generated inside its nuclear fuel rods. These are sealed metal rods containing pellets made of uranium oxide, a radioactive substance. Reactions from the nuclear fission (see box opposite) create the energy that heats the water.

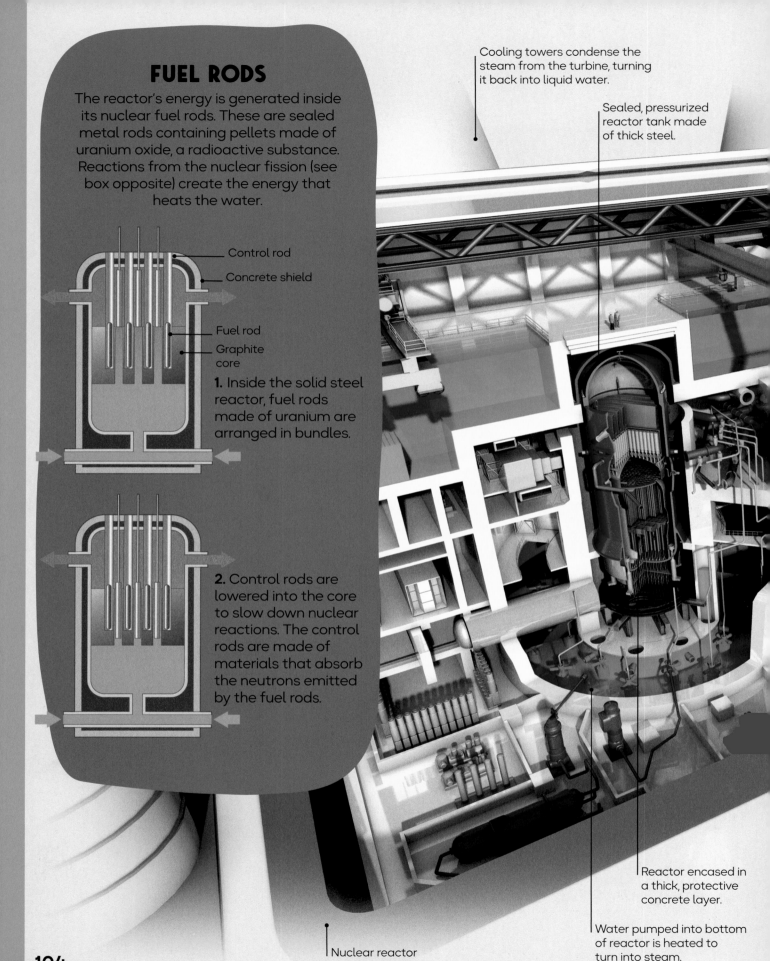

Control rod

Concrete shield

Fuel rod

Graphite core

1. Inside the solid steel reactor, fuel rods made of uranium are arranged in bundles.

2. Control rods are lowered into the core to slow down nuclear reactions. The control rods are made of materials that absorb the neutrons emitted by the fuel rods.

Cooling towers condense the steam from the turbine, turning it back into liquid water.

Sealed, pressurized reactor tank made of thick steel.

Reactor encased in a thick, protective concrete layer.

Water pumped into bottom of reactor is heated to turn into steam.

Nuclear reactor containment building

104

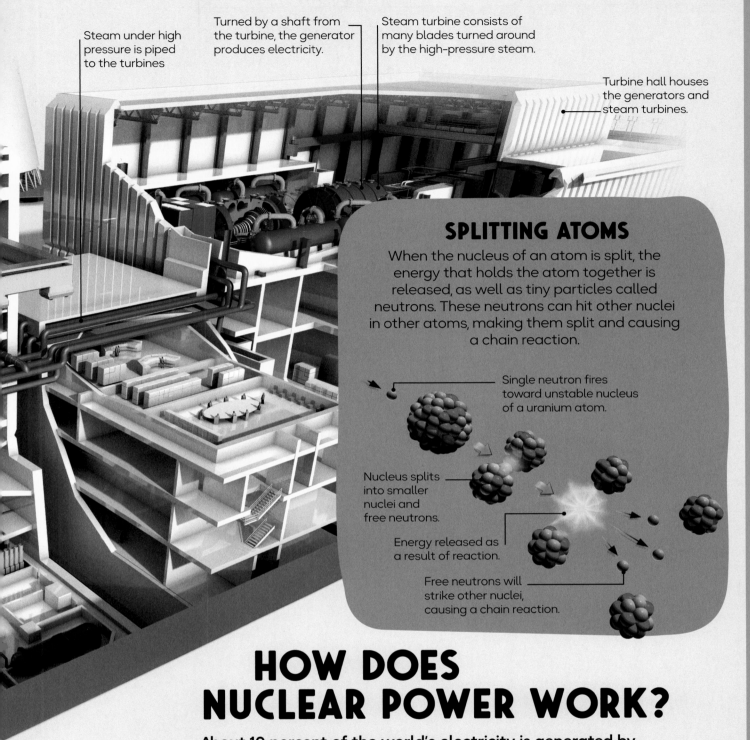

Steam under high pressure is piped to the turbines

Turned by a shaft from the turbine, the generator produces electricity.

Steam turbine consists of many blades turned around by the high-pressure steam.

Turbine hall houses the generators and steam turbines.

SPLITTING ATOMS

When the nucleus of an atom is split, the energy that holds the atom together is released, as well as tiny particles called neutrons. These neutrons can hit other nuclei in other atoms, making them split and causing a chain reaction.

Single neutron fires toward unstable nucleus of a uranium atom.

Nucleus splits into smaller nuclei and free neutrons.

Energy released as a result of reaction.

Free neutrons will strike other nuclei, causing a chain reaction.

HOW DOES NUCLEAR POWER WORK?

About 10 percent of the world's electricity is generated by nuclear power plants. These use the energy created by splitting the nucleus of atoms (a process called nuclear fission) to drive giant electricity-generating turbines.

A nuclear power plant is made up of a large reactor, steam-driven turbines, and electricity generators all connected via numerous control and safety systems. Many nuclear power stations are situated on the coast so that seawater can be used in their cooling processes.

Nuclear power plants rely on a chain reaction within their fuel rods to generate huge amounts of energy. This energy heats water into steam that drives turbines. The turbines, in turn, power electricity generators. Electricity is carried to where it is needed by power lines. Nuclear power is reliable and—unlike power plants fueled by coal or oil—does not emit polluting gases into the atmosphere. But fears remain about accidents that may cause radioactive leaks harmful to living things.

HOW DO WIND FARMS WORK?

A wind farm is a collection of wind turbines that may be grouped together on land or out at sea. Each wind turbine uses the power of the wind to turn its propeller-like rotor blades in order to generate electricity.

Wind farms may be small or large collections of wind turbines. Thornsea Project One is located off the Yorkshire Coast in England, for example, and comprises 174 turbines. The turbines themselves can vary in size—from small models suitable for a single house to giants standing almost 660 ft. (200m) tall and with a rotor diameter of 584 ft. (178m). Large wind turbines can be expensive to build and some people object to their spoiling of the landscape or generating a lot of noise. However, wind energy will not run out and can generate electricity cheaply and cleanly without creating harmful emissions that pollute the atmosphere.

A large group of wind turbines form a wind farm in the ocean. Automatic controllers inside each turbine monitor the wind speed and weather conditions, and may shut the turbine down if the wind reaches dangerously high speeds.

Tall tower made out of steel, concrete, or a combination of both.

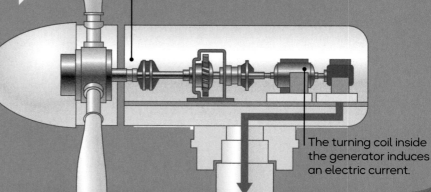

Incoming wind direction

Rotor blades turn, spinning a central shaft that runs through a gearbox.

GENERATORS

Generators make electricity by turning a wire coil through a magnetic field. A wind turbine provides the mechanical turning power for the generator via its rotor blades, which are moved by the wind.

The turning coil inside the generator induces an electric current.

DIFFERENT DESIGNS

Wind turbines come in different shapes and designs. Some have blades that turn on a vertical axis instead of horizontally. These may generate less electricity but they take up less space and can operate closer to the ground, like these colorful Savonius turbines in a city park.

Curved blades catch the wind and spin, turning the turbine to generate electricity.

Anemometer measures wind speed.

The blades and the turbine body, called the nacelle, turn to point into the wind.

Generator inside the turbine generates electricity.

Angle of each rotor blade, called its pitch, can be adjusted depending on the wind's direction.

HOW CAN WE BE MORE ENERGY EFFICIENT?

Energy efficiency is about using less energy overall to perform tasks. In the home, improved energy efficiency can be achieved by using less power-hungry devices and by reducing heat loss from a building.

Rising energy costs and concern about the potential harm to the planet caused by certain types of energy has seen more homes adopt energy-efficient technology or practices. Fitting more energy-efficient lights and electrical appliances, reducing central heating temperatures, and turning off electrical items when not in use all help to reduce energy use, as can insulating roofs and walls to stop heat from escaping. Along with energy efficiency, more and more people are using renewable energies such as solar and wind power as well as geothermal power (heat from Earth). These are forms of energy that do not release harmful emissions into the atmosphere and will not run out.

Roof is covered in grass, which helps insulate house and reduce heat loss.

Solar panels are made up of a series of photovoltaic cells that generate electricity from sunlight.

Windows are triple glazed to stop heat from leaking out.

SOLAR POWER

Photovoltaic cells are made up of semiconducting materials, such as silicon, that release electrons when struck by light. These electrons flow as a current that can be used by an electrical circuit to power electrical devices.

Light rays strike panel

Each cell generates a small electric voltage between two semiconductors.

Solar panel contains many photovoltaic cells.

Electric current flows through wiring to light bulb.

This innovative eco-home is a passive house, meaning that it generates its own energy and does not take electricity from the supply grid. It is built into the ground, which helps keep warmth in.

Domestic wind turbine generates enough electricity to light the house.

LOW-ENERGY LIGHT BULB

Compact fluorescent lamps (CFLs) generate light by passing electricity through a tube full o These gases give off ultraviolet light, which causes a phosphor coating on the tube to shine. CFLs last longer and use a fraction of the energy used by traditional light bulbs.

Phosphor coating on tube emits light.

Spiraling tube contains argon and mercury gases.

Thick plastic foam between the outer and inner walls helps keep warmth in the house.

Ballast produces an electric current that flows through the tube.

Fitting for light bulb socket

Underfloor heating system uses heat obtained from the geothermal piping.

Geothermal piping full of liquid draws in heat from the soil.

HEAT LOSS

This heat image of a house glows orange where heat energy loss is at its greatest. The windows and roof are well insulated, but most heat is lost through the poorly insulated walls.

This type of bridge is built outward from each vertical tower. To complete the span, a central beam connects each arm.

Forth Rail Bridge, Scotland
(built 1883–1890)

The Millau Viaduct is a cable-stayed bridge. It looks similar to a suspension bridge, but the roadbed is supported by the masts, not by anchors at each end.

Concrete towers rose at a rate of 13 ft. (4m) per day.

Temporary towers were taken down at the end.

Hydraulic jacks pushed the temporary towers up 3 ft. (1m) at a time.

HOW IS A SUPERBRIDGE BUILT?

Today, lightweight steel and other extrastrong materials allow engineers to build enormous bridges that span rivers, valleys, and seas. The Millau Viaduct in France is a record breaker—the tallest bridge ever built.

Opened in 2004, the viaduct took ten years to plan and three to build, at a cost of $405 million. First, seven giant, reinforced concrete towers were built up from the valley floor. Next, hydraulic jacks and wedges pushed out steel decks for carrying the road from each side of the valley—1.2 in. (3cm) at a time. Temporary steel towers were built between the concrete ones to reduce the distance over which the roadbed had to be supported. Finally, the temporary towers were taken down.

SUSPENSION BRIDGE

In this type of bridge, the cables are attached to massive anchorages at each end. These support the weight of the roadbed.

Golden Gate Bridge, San Francisco (built 1933–1937)

The tallest mast top is 1,125 ft. (343m) above the river—higher than the top of the Eiffel Tower in Paris, France.

ARCH BRIDGE

This is one of the oldest bridge designs. The weight is carried down the arch to massive supports at each end.

Sydney Harbour Bridge, Australia (built 1923–1932)

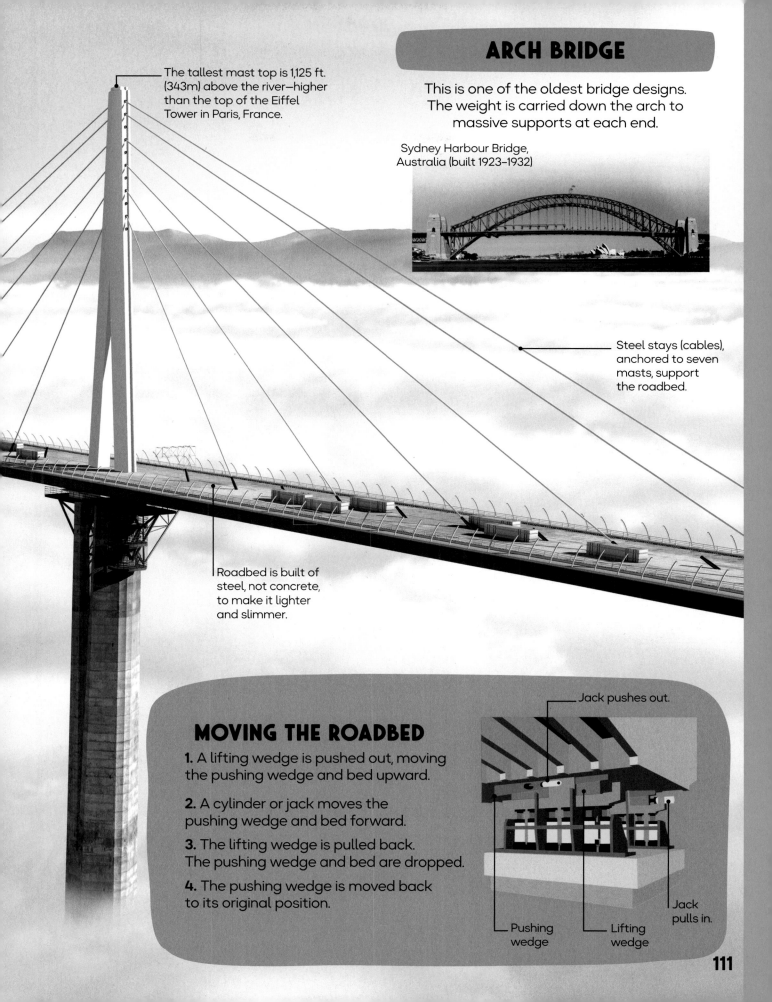

Steel stays (cables), anchored to seven masts, support the roadbed.

Roadbed is built of steel, not concrete, to make it lighter and slimmer.

MOVING THE ROADBED

1. A lifting wedge is pushed out, moving the pushing wedge and bed upward.

2. A cylinder or jack moves the pushing wedge and bed forward.

3. The lifting wedge is pulled back. The pushing wedge and bed are dropped.

4. The pushing wedge is moved back to its original position.

Jack pushes out.

Pushing wedge

Lifting wedge

Jack pulls in.

TUNNEL LINING

After tunnels are bored or cut out, their walls have to be reinforced quickly before they collapse, usually with a framework made of steel and a lining made of concrete. The tunnel is then finished with fittings, such as a roadway or railroad tracks, and with lighting and safety systems.

A machine spreads concrete in the Gotthard Base Tunnel in Switzerland.

Prefabricated, curved concrete walls support the newly bored tunnel.

Conveyor belts powered by electric motors carry rock chips away from the tunnel boring machine.

HOW ARE TUNNELS BUILT?

Tunnels are used to carry large quantities of water from reservoirs to cities. They also provide trains and motor vehicles with quick, convenient routes through hills and mountains, under seas and rivers, and beneath cities.

Before boring a tunnel, engineers analyze soil and rock samples and drill test holes to investigate the ground they are about to dig through. Some shallow tunnels are built using a cut and cover method where a "U"-shaped trench is dug and then a strong roof fitted over it, turning it into a tunnel. Many larger and deeper tunnels are now built using gigantic tunnel boring machines (TBMs). These giant, cylinder-shaped machines are lowered into the first part of a tunnel shaft and then slowly creep forward

Hydraulic rams (powerful pistons) push the cutter head into the rock face.

A giant tunnel boring machine (TBM) works inside the Gotthard Base Tunnel underneath the Swiss Alps. The tunnel is in fact a pair of 35-mi.- (57-km-) long tunnels. They are the world's longest and deepest railroad tunnels.

TBMs limit the disturbance to the surrounding ground and produce a smooth tunnel wall.

CUTTING HEAD

A TBM with a cutting head 20 ft. (6m) in diameter breaks through the rock after boring a tunnel in Bangalore, India. This tunnel forms a part of the 26.2-mi.- (42.3-km-) long Bangalore Metro system, called Namma Metro.

Powerful pneumatic jacks can be raised or lowered to alter the direction of tunneling.

Tunnel workers are dwarfed by a giant TBM that cuts the tunnel at a typical rate of 28 in. (70cm) per hour.

Cutting head is fitted with sharp, tough, steel cutting disks that cause fractures in the rock face and chip it away.

Rock chips travel through gaps in the rotating cutting head and are carried back from the TBM for collection by other machines.

HOW DO HIGH-SPEED TRAINS RUN?

The first high-speed train service in the world was the Shinkansen, opened in Japan in 1960. Since that time, similar trains, some able to travel at speeds of up to 373 mph (600km/h), have entered service in other parts of Asia and Europe.

High-speed trains are all electric—obtaining their power from electrified rails below or from power cables running above the railroad line. This electricity powers a series of electric motors to propel the train rapidly without it needing to carry heavy, bulky fuel such as diesel. At higher speeds, all vehicles face resistance from the air they pass through. The front of a high-speed train is designed to be streamlined so that it cuts through the air as smoothly as possible.

A TGV (Train à Grande Vitesse) high-speed train races through France, reaching a top speed of 200 mph (320km/h) at some points on its route. The TGV-M, an even faster and more energy-efficient train, is set to enter service in 2024.

OVERHEAD POWER

A Pendolino tilting train tilts so that it can round curves in the track without slowing down. Many electric trains rely on power cables directly above the track to provide them with electricity.

Headlights and warning lights on the front of the train.

03

Steel track precisely made to help the train travel as smoothly as possible.

MAGLEV

Maglev (magnetic levitation) trains use powerful electromagnets that repel each other to lift the train above the track, called a guideway. Further electromagnets along the side of the guideway attract the train, pulling it forward. The fastest Maglev trains travel at speeds of up to 373 mph (600km/h).

Propulsion magnets along side of guideway propel train forward.

Guideway magnet repels train magnet.

Electromagnets repel each other, causing train to float above guideway.

Train driver in crash-protected cab monitors engine computers and signals.

Main transformer weighs 8.8 tons and converts the voltage down to 1,500 volts for the train's engine.

Pantograph receives 25,000 volts of electricity from the overhead power line.

Motor bogie uses two 1,000 horsepower electric motors to turn wheels.

HOW DO SUBMARINES DIVE?

Submarines are built so that they can float in water or dive below the surface. They do this by means of large ballast tanks that are wrapped around their hull (body). These can be filled with water or air in order to change the submarine's weight.

When a submarine's ballast tanks are filled with air, it is lighter in weight than the water it displaces (pushes out of its way) and so it rises upward. To dive, the tanks are filled with water so that the submarine becomes heavier and sinks. Once the submarine reaches the desired depth, water is blown out of special ballast tanks, called negative tanks, to make the submarine weigh the same amount as the water it displaces. The submarine will then float under the water and can cruise along, changing direction using one or more flaps called rudders on its tail.

An Ohio Class submarine used by the U.S. Navy is 560 ft. (170m) long and can weigh more than 20,670 tons when submerged. Powered by a nuclear reactor, this giant sub can travel on missions lasting up to three months.

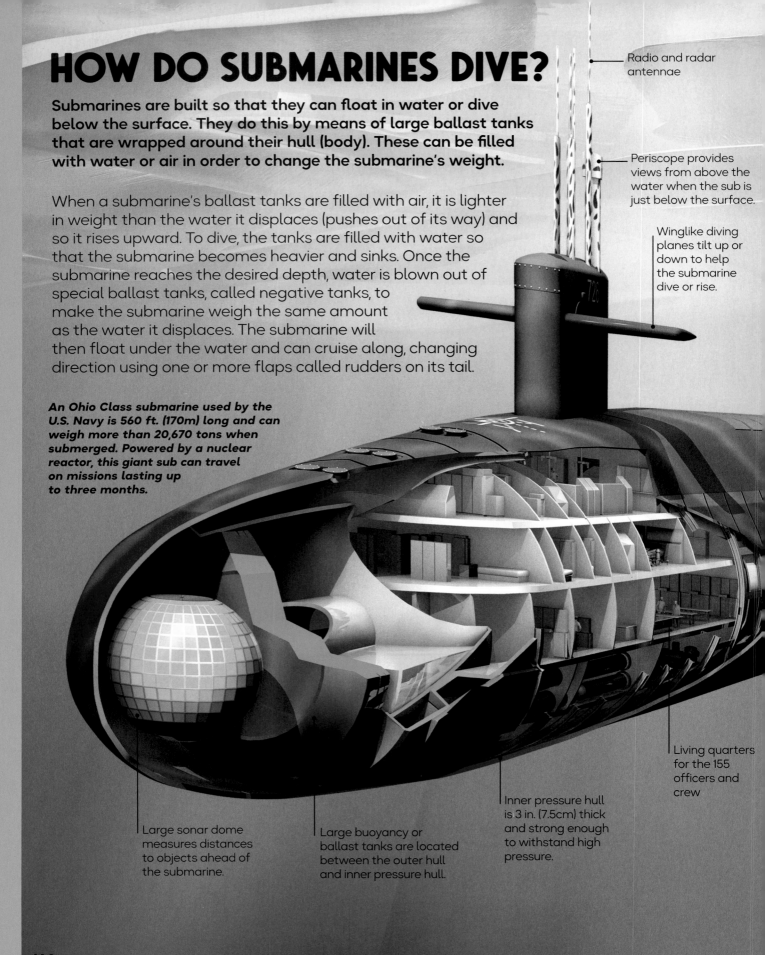

Radio and radar antennae

Periscope provides views from above the water when the sub is just below the surface.

Winglike diving planes tilt up or down to help the submarine dive or rise.

Living quarters for the 155 officers and crew

Inner pressure hull is 3 in. (7.5cm) thick and strong enough to withstand high pressure.

Large buoyancy or ballast tanks are located between the outer hull and inner pressure hull.

Large sonar dome measures distances to objects ahead of the submarine.

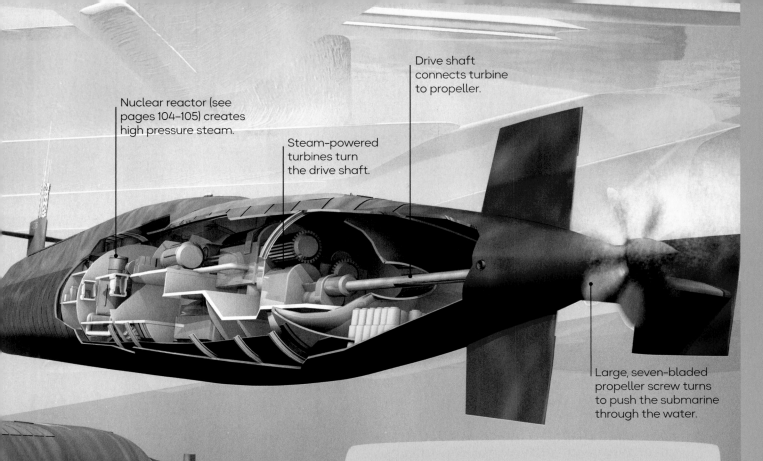

Nuclear reactor (see pages 104–105) creates high pressure steam.

Steam-powered turbines turn the drive shaft.

Drive shaft connects turbine to propeller.

Large, seven-bladed propeller screw turns to push the submarine through the water.

SUBMERSIBLE

An ultra-deep submersible can reach a depth of up to 3,280 ft. (11,000m) in approximately three hours. The manned vehicle allows scientists and researchers to explore the deepest parts of the ocean.

GOING UP, GOING DOWN

A submarine uses large ballast tanks surrounding its interior to control its buoyancy. These tanks can be flooded with water to make the sub heavier so that it will sink. To surface, compressed air forces the water out of the tanks.

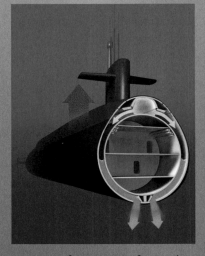

1. To surface, air is forced through the sub's tanks, pushing the water out. As air fills the tanks the submarine rises to the surface.

2. To dive, the sub's lower tank valves are opened. Water fills the tanks, making the submarine heavier and allowing it to descend.

HOW DO JET ENGINES WORK?

A jet engine is a type of internal combustion engine that generates thrust out of its rear exhaust to propel it forward. Jet engines are found on many airliners and fast military aircraft and, occasionally, on record-breaking fast cars.

Cold air is drawn into the front of a jet engine and then squeezed by a series of turning turbine blades to increase its pressure and its temperature. The air then enters the combustion chamber where it is mixed with fuel and burned, reaching temperatures of about 1,650°F (900°C). Large amounts of hot gases are produced and expand out of the back of the combustion chamber and the rear exhaust nozzle. The force of these rapidly expanding gases creates an equal force in the opposite direction, thrusting the aircraft or land vehicle forward.

Smooth engine covering is called a nacelle. The engines burn about 5 gal. (18L) of fuel per second

Nose cap

Parachutes to float the booster safely back to Earth.

Large air "intakes" channel air into the jet engine.

SOLID-FUEL ROCKET

Some rocket engines are fueled by a ready-mixed combination of solid fuel and oxidizer (an oxygen-producing substance). The two solid rocket boosters (SRBs) used on the former space shuttle carried about 550 tons of fuel and provided more than 80 percent of the Shuttle's thrust at liftoff. Within two minutes, all of their fuel was used up.

Small motors fire up to remove SRB from the space shuttle.

Igniter sets light to solid fuel and oxidizer mixture.

Long, tapering nose is designed to slice through the air and keep drag to a minimum.

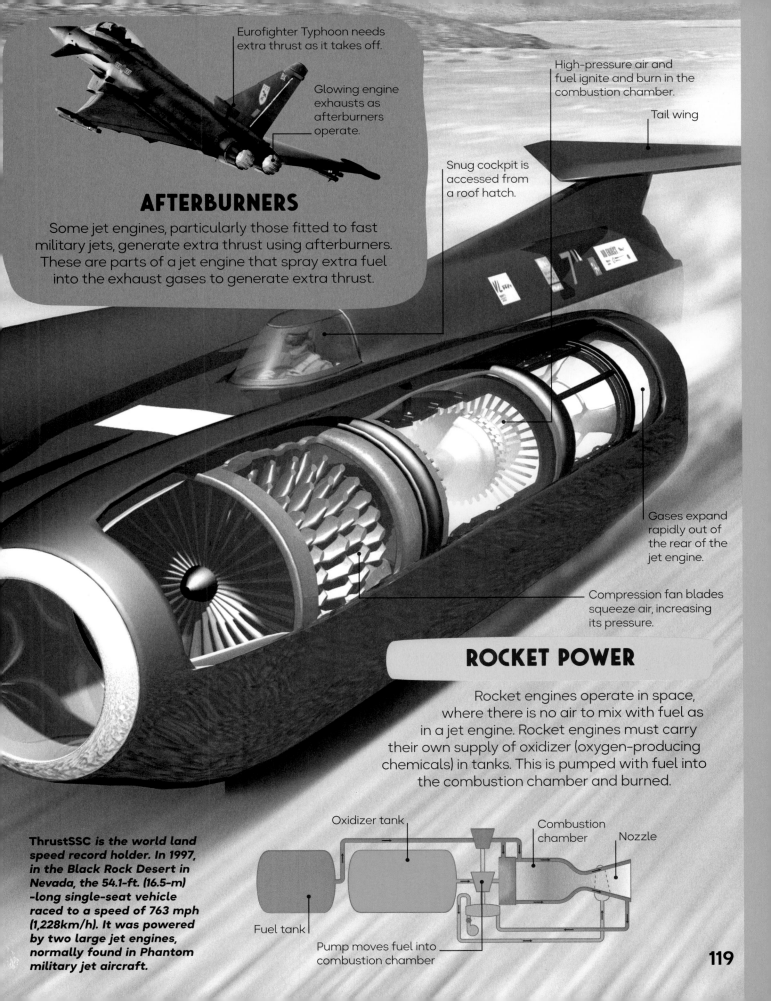

Eurofighter Typhoon needs extra thrust as it takes off.

Glowing engine exhausts as afterburners operate.

High-pressure air and fuel ignite and burn in the combustion chamber.

Tail wing

Snug cockpit is accessed from a roof hatch.

AFTERBURNERS

Some jet engines, particularly those fitted to fast military jets, generate extra thrust using afterburners. These are parts of a jet engine that spray extra fuel into the exhaust gases to generate extra thrust.

Gases expand rapidly out of the rear of the jet engine.

Compression fan blades squeeze air, increasing its pressure.

ROCKET POWER

Rocket engines operate in space, where there is no air to mix with fuel as in a jet engine. Rocket engines must carry their own supply of oxidizer (oxygen-producing chemicals) in tanks. This is pumped with fuel into the combustion chamber and burned.

ThrustSSC is the world land speed record holder. In 1997, in the Black Rock Desert in Nevada, the 54.1-ft. (16.5-m) -long single-seat vehicle raced to a speed of 763 mph (1,228km/h). It was powered by two large jet engines, normally found in Phantom military jet aircraft.

Oxidizer tank

Combustion chamber

Nozzle

Fuel tank

Pump moves fuel into combustion chamber

119

HOW ARE THINGS LAUNCHED INTO SPACE?

A rocket's payload is the cargo that it carries into space. This could be a space capsule containing astronauts or a communications satellite that will orbit Earth. Launching a payload into space requires vast amounts of thrust from rocket engines.

A launch vehicle's giant rocket engines need huge amounts of fuel and oxidizer. The *Falcon 9* rocket's first stage has nine engines, which at full power use 3,200 lb. (1450kg) of fuel and liquid oxygen per second. Fuel, oxidizer, and engines are extremely heavy to carry into space, so two methods are used, sometimes together. Booster rockets provide extra thrust at lift-off, but then fall away once their fuel is used up. The now lighter launch vehicle needs less thrust to power it. Some launch vehicles have two or three stages, each with their own rocket engines. Once a stage has finished powering the vehicle, it falls away to reduce the rocket's overall weight, and the next stage's engine fires and takes over.

— Dragon space craft

— The second stage falls back to Earth and burns up in the atmosphere.

— The interstage connects the first and second stage.

— The *Falcon 9*'s first stage is reusable. It deploys landing legs as it falls back to Earth, then is collected and cleaned to be used again.

— Landing legs allow first stage to land back on Earth.

The Falcon 9 is a reusable, two-stage rocket. In November 2020, it launched the Crew Dragon space craft Resilience on its mission to the International Space Station. The mission lasted for 167 days, and Resilience landed back on Earth in May 2021.

TYPES OF ORBITS

Satellites can be put into different types of orbits around Earth or another body in space.

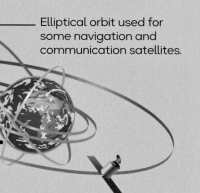

Low Earth orbit used for weather and spy satellites.

Elliptical orbit used for some navigation and communication satellites.

Polar orbit used for weather and land-imaging satellites.

Geosynchronous orbit used for communications and navigation.

The nose cone protects the capsule during the flight.

Astronauts sit in the crew module.

The trunk holds the cargo.

The Crew Dragon is a type of Dragon 2 space craft made by SpaceX which is partially reusable, just like the Falcon 9 rocket.

LOOKING DOWN

Many satellites launched into space follow a circular or elliptical path as they orbit Earth. They perform a range of useful tasks, from tracking storms to taking satellite images of Earth (below).

ION THRUSTER

An alternative form of thrust can be provided by an ion thruster. This generates thrust by accelerating ions (electrically charged atoms or molecules). It is weaker than thrusters that use fuel and oxidizer, but lasts longer, and can propel vehicles to greater speeds.

HOW IS A SPACE STATION BUILT?

Space stations are large spacecraft that are designed to stay in space for a long period of time. They contain living quarters for crews of astronauts and have one or more docking ports so that other spacecraft can arrive and leave.

Two astronauts perform an extravehicular activity (a spacewalk) to complete tasks on the exterior of the ISS.

The first space stations, such as NASA's *Skylab* and the Soviet Union's *Salyut 1,* were single units built on Earth and carried into space by large launch vehicles. The *Mir* space station in the 1980s was the first to be constructed out of a number of separate modules, each sent into space via a separate launch vehicle. The construction of the International Space Station (ISS) began in 1998 and is the ultimate in modular design. Assembled over the course of more than 120 spaceflights, the space station consists of a long truss to which giant solar panels, modules, docking ports, and nodes, which connect different parts of the station to one another, are all attached.

The ISS is 358 ft (109m) wide and on Earth would weigh more than 463 tons (420,000kg).

LIVING IN SPACE

The ISS has been lived in continuously since 2000. Crews tend to spend three to six months on board before being swapped over via a docking spacecraft that may also bring new experiments, equipment, food, and other supplies.

ROBOTIC ARM

Robotic arms are used on the ISS to handle modules and parts. This Canadarm 2 robotic arm performs maintenance checks and moves supplies and rubbish. The European Robotic Arm was launched in 2021 and transports astronauts from one site to another. Its cameras to inspect the outside of the space station.

The ISS makes 16 orbits of Earth every day, at altitudes of between 205 to 255 mi. (330 to 410km).

Module fitted to the space station contains a laboratory and large numbers of space experiments.

PLSS (primary life support subsystem) backpack supplies oxygen to the astronaut and electrical power to the suit.

Helmet contains radio for communication with other astronauts.

Crater is approximately 2,400 ft. (730m) wide.

The Rosalind Franklin rover (known previously as the ExoMars rover) is a robot planned to arrive on Mars in 2022. It will navigate its own way around the planet's surface and use a drill and onboard mini chemistry lab to analyze samples of soil and rock to search for signs of present or past life forms.

Orbiting and fly-by space probes take many digital images of a body's surface from above. These are then relayed to Earth and examined by scientists. This image is from the Mars Reconnaissance Orbiter and shows an impact crater on Mars.

Twin cameras enable the rover to build up a 3-D map of the ground ahead.

Solar panels power the robot by generating electricity from sunlight.

Antenna can send and receive data and instructions via radio waves.

Controller inside body helps plot the best route forward for the rover, avoiding large obstacles.

Each wheel can be steered independently by the rover.

Drillbox able to drill holes into the planet's surface, up to 6.5 ft. (2m) deep.

124

HOW DO MACHINES EXPLORE PLANETS?

Space probes are uncrewed machines that are sent into space to explore other planets in the solar system, as well as moons, the Sun, asteroids, and comets. They use radio signals to send back digital images and measurements made with scientific instruments.

Probes are launched from Earth by rocket-powered launch vehicles and are sent on carefully calculated flight paths to their target. Their journeys may take many years. The *Cassini-Huygens* space probe took seven years to reach Saturn. Some probes fly by different planets or moons on the way to their main target. The *Voyager 2* probe, for example, performed fly-bys of Jupiter, Saturn, Uranus, and Neptune. Other probes go into orbit around their target and may drop a separate lander probe onto a planet or a moon. Some lander probes stay in the one place, while others are mobile rovers that can trundle across the surface and analyze the rock and soil using scientific instruments.

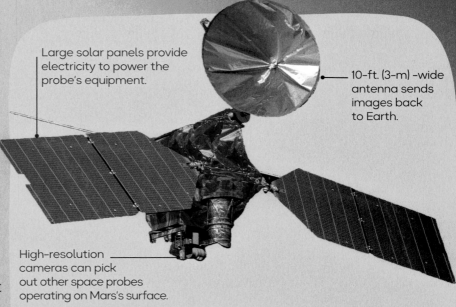

Large solar panels provide electricity to power the probe's equipment.

10-ft. (3-m) -wide antenna sends images back to Earth.

High-resolution cameras can pick out other space probes operating on Mars's surface.

ORBITERS

Probes such as this Mars Reconnaissance Orbiter (MRO) go into orbit around their target. Their scientific instruments may measure the atmosphere, weather, and surface. The MRO orbits Mars every 112 minutes and uses high-resolution cameras to photograph every part of the planet's surface.

TOUCHDOWN!

Getting a probe to reach the surface of a planet, comet, or moon can be tricky, and many probes have been lost on their descent. In 2005, the *Huygens* probe successfully landed on one of Saturn's moons, Titan, more than 745,000 mi. (1.2 billion km) away from Earth. Beneath the haze of Titan's atmosphere, the probe discovered a world of dunes and rocks, with seas of liquid methane.

1. Heat shield protected probe as it traveled through Titan's thick atmosphere.

2. Parachute opened to slow down probe and the heat shield was jettisoned.

3. Probe gathered information about Titan's atmosphere and surface, as it descended and for 90 minutes after it landed.

HOW WOULD A CREWED BASE ON THE MOON WORK?

It has been more than 50 years since a human astronaut has set foot on the Moon, but many think that humans will return to the Moon in the future, possibly living in a dedicated base on its surface.

A permanent base on the Moon might allow scientists to build and operate radio telescopes and other scientific instruments free of the distortion and pollution of Earth's atmosphere. Uncrewed reusable spacecraft could ferry supplies to the base regularly, taking less than three days to travel from Earth to the Moon. Their return journey, carrying back valuable materials mined or processed on the Moon, would use less power and fuel because the Moon's gravity is only about one-sixth of Earth's. This means that less thrust is required to lift off from the lunar surface and head home to Earth or on missions farther afield to other parts of the solar system.

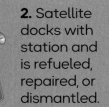

Robotic servicer

Satellite

1. Uncrewed space station contains fuel tanks to service docking spacecraft.

2. Satellite docks with station and is refueled, repaired, or dismantled.

REFUELING

In the future, space stations may be built to refuel spacecraft on their journeys to and from the Moon or beyond. They will be fitted with docking ports for spacecraft to latch onto, while their tanks are filled with fuel. Satellites may also be captured and refueled to extend their working lives.

The six-person "crew" of the Mars-500 experiment emerge after 520 days.

MARS-500

Crewed missions to Mars may involve a journey of up to 18 months, using the Moon as a launch platform. The Mars-500 experiment simulated living in a spacecraftlike environment to test the effects of a long space journey on humans.

Moonbase built into the lunar surface, which helps insulate the structures.

Large robotic arm grips and moves rocks and other large objects.

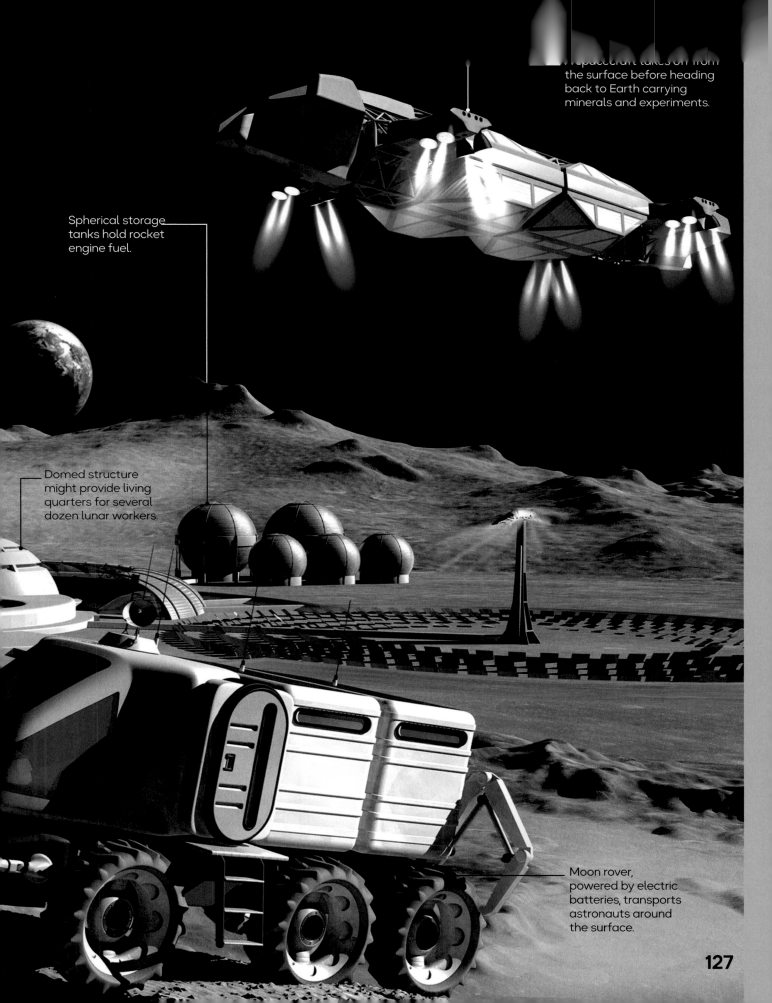

Spherical storage tanks hold rocket engine fuel.

A spacecraft takes off from the surface before heading back to Earth carrying minerals and experiments.

Domed structure might provide living quarters for several dozen lunar workers.

Moon rover, powered by electric batteries, transports astronauts around the surface.

127

SCIENCE AND TECHNOLOGY
FIND OUT MORE ABOUT HOW THE WORLD WORKS

WEBSITES TO VISIT

https://kids.kiddle.co/Robot
Discover more about robots, from the first ones ever made to the ones of the future.

http://science.howstuffworks.com/nanotechnology.htm
Learn more about nanotechnology at the How Stuff Works website.

www.darvill.clara.net/altenerg/nuclear.htm
Get a lot of detail about all kinds of energy sources, from nuclear power to wind power, at this informative website.

https://kids.britannica.com/kids/article/nuclear-energy/353549
Read this brief guide to how nuclear power works and what it can be used for.

www.pbs.org/wgbh/nova/bridge/
Learn how to survey land and select the right bridge type for different situations at these web pages presented by PBS.

https://kids.kiddle.co/Submarine
Read about the history of submarines, the marvel of modern submarines, and view images of underwater submersibles.

www.nasa.gov/audience/forstudents/k-4/stories/nasa-knows/what-is-a-rocket-k4.html
Learn more about how rockets work in this guide from NASA.

www.esa.int/kids/en/learn/Technology/Useful_space/Satellites
Read about satellites and their different jobs at the European Space Agency website.

www.spacekids.co.uk/spacesuits/
See how spacesuits for astronauts performing spacewalks have developed over time.

www.nasa.gov/mission_pages/station/main/index.html
Find out all you want to know about the International Space Station at NASA's detailed web pages on the giant orbiting satellite.

CHAPTER FIVE
HISTORY

HOW WERE THE EARLIEST TOWNS FORMED?

About 10,000 years ago, peoples who had previously wandered and hunted for their food began to grow crops and domesticate animals. As they started settling in one place, villages developed, some of which would expand to become the first towns and cities.

As early peoples became more skilled at farming, they created surpluses of food that they began to trade with others. This need for markets saw some of the first settlements form close to the farmers' fields and often near rivers. As these settlements grew larger, services were established for the inhabitants to use, such as stores, water supplies, and harbors for boats. Soon, some people developed other skills besides farming and became metalworkers and toolmakers. People also gathered together in early towns to defend themselves from other, hostile, groups. Some of these towns built protective surrounding walls.

Located on the banks of the Euphrates River in present-day Iraq, the city of Ur was founded almost 6,000 years ago. A settlement of the Sumerian civilization, it featured public buildings, including temples and markets, with houses on its outskirts.

TOWN ON STILTS

In the third millennium B.C., while the Egyptians were building pyramids, the Celtic people of Europe lived in fortified villages. Many were on riverbanks where they could easily be defended. The wooden houses were surrounded by a high wooden fence or stockade.

Thatched, straw roofs with a gap to let out the smoke.

Houses built on stilts to protect against seasonal floods.

Pathways made of split logs.

Temple walls made of mud bricks and measuring approximately 150 ft. (45m) wide and 215 ft. (65m) long.

The Ziggurat of Ur, dedicated to the moon god, Nanna, is the largest temple in the city.

MOHENJO-DARO

The ruins of this ancient city, located in the Indus Valley of Pakistan, were rediscovered in 1921. At its peak, as many as 35,000 people may have lived in the city, making it one of the largest ancient cities in the world.

A religious ceremony is performed inside the temple walls.

People buy animals, food, and goods to trade in the town market.

Oxen used to pull simple wooden carts.

HOW WERE MUMMIES MADE?

Mummies are bodies that have been preserved so that they do not decay. Many civilizations created mummies, including the Egyptians. They believed that preserving a body after death would allow the soul to survive in the afterlife. Some Egyptian mummies have survived intact for more than 5,000 years.

Rituals surrounded all stages of mummification. The process began with washing the body. Key organs were then removed and preserved before being placed in special ceremonial containers called canopic jars. The heart was left inside the body because the Egyptians believed it would be weighed in the afterlife to determine whether a person had led a good life. After being packed with salts and left on a table to dry out, the body would be washed again and covered in oils, and artificial eyes would be added to the head. Once the mummy was complete, the funeral ceremony could be held.

COFFINS

This shows the mummy of an Egyptian queen, complete with a painted death mask, being placed inside an elaborate coffin. A priest would recite spells from the Book of the Dead to protect the queen on her journey to the afterlife.

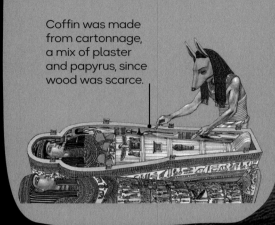

Coffin was made from cartonnage, a mix of plaster and papyrus, since wood was scarce.

PREPARING A MUMMY

The mummification process took about 70 days. For 40 days, the body was left to dry after being packed with natron salt crystals. The salt absorbed the moisture from the body and prevented it from decay. Only when the body was dry could the wrapping process begin.

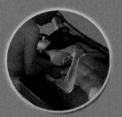

1. Body is washed and purified with palm wine.

2. Stomach is removed, followed by the lungs, intestines, and liver.

3. A hook inserted up the nostrils is used to scrape out the brain.

4. Body is washed free of natron salt and then oiled.

5. Body is stuffed with leaves, linen, and sawdust.

Body is covered in oils and perfumes.

Embalmers work to mummify an Egyptian king in an embalming tent close to the site of his tob. They wrap the body in layers of linen bandages and use resin from trees to stick together the linen wrappings.

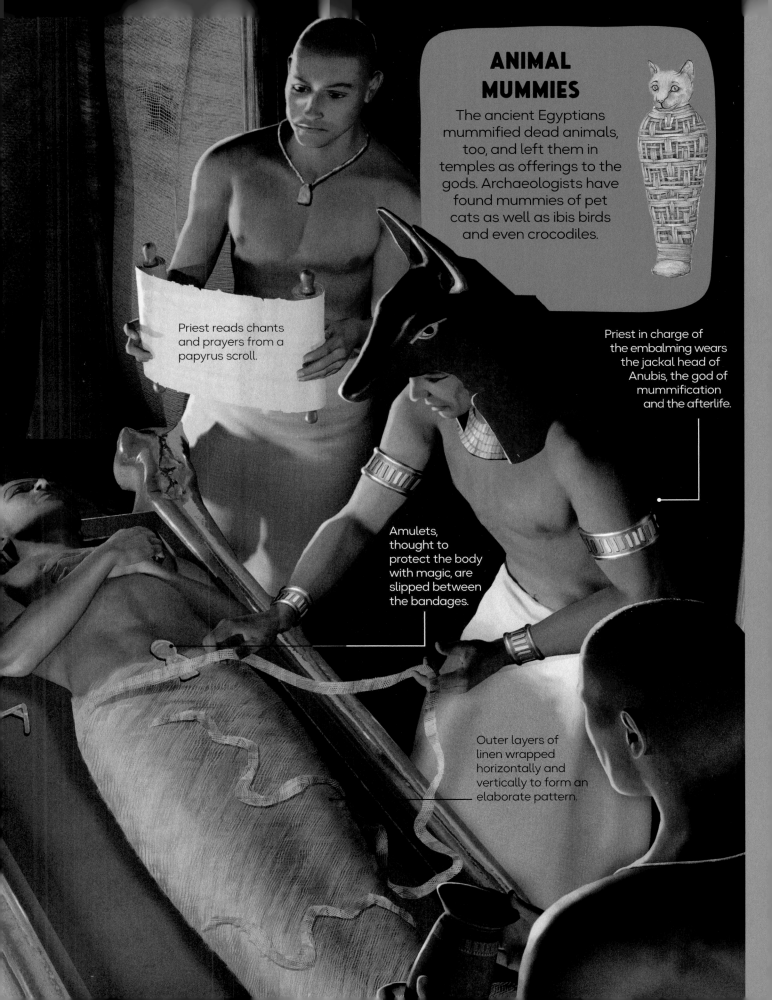

ANIMAL MUMMIES

The ancient Egyptians mummified dead animals, too, and left them in temples as offerings to the gods. Archaeologists have found mummies of pet cats as well as ibis birds and even crocodiles.

Priest reads chants and prayers from a papyrus scroll.

Priest in charge of the embalming wears the jackal head of Anubis, the god of mummification and the afterlife.

Amulets, thought to protect the body with magic, are slipped between the bandages.

Outer layers of linen wrapped horizontally and vertically to form an elaborate pattern.

HOW DID EGYPTIANS WRITE?

The ancient Egyptians recorded a lot of information about their daily lives—from the details of harvests and taxes, to letters, royal orders, and prayers. Over time, they developed a number of different scripts. The most famous was the hieroglyphic script, a form of picture writing developed more than 5,000 years ago.

Hieroglyphs used images to represent objects and, later, certain sounds, so that information could be written down, stored, and communicated. This work was done by trained scribes. Scribes supervised the carving of hieroglyphs into stone, but they themselves mostly wrote on pieces of pottery called ostraca, or on papyrus. This was made from the flattened strips of marsh reeds, pressed, and dried to form long sheets. A scribe would write with a brush of frayed river reeds, dipped in an ink made from soot or rocky minerals ground down and mixed with liquid.

The Great Temple of Amun in Karnak was an enormous ceremonial center on the banks of the Nile River. It was altered and expanded over many centuries by around 30 different pharaohs. Its pillars and walls were richly decorated in hieroglyphs.

A pharaoh's name is written inside an oval frame called a cartouche. _____

Outer rind of the papyrus stem is peeled away.

Inner pith is cut into strips and laid out in a layer.

A second, horizontal layer is flattened over the first and dried.

PAPYRUS

The reed's fibers made the papyrus scroll stronger than paper, and many scrolls have survived. This triangular-stemmed plant grew in abundance along the Nile River and was used to make boats, baskets, sandals, and writing material.

A hieroglyph showing the _____ ankh—a symbol of life.

HIEROGLYPHS

Hieroglyphs were used for more than 3,000 years before they fell into disuse. It was only in the 1800s that the meaning of the different characters, numbering more than 2,000, was deciphered.

The pylon, or gateway, into the main hall of the temple.

Hieroglyphs carved into stone pillars and painted in bright colors.

HOW WERE PYRAMIDS BUILT?

A pyramid is a structure with four triangular sides sloping inward to a point. A number of civilizations built pyramids as religious temples. The most famous pyramids are those built by the ancient Egyptians as tombs for their pharaohs (kings).

Of the 100 or so pyramid ruins in Egypt, the Great Pyramid in Giza is the largest. It was built for the pharaoh Cheops (Khufu) in about 2500 B.C. and consists of as many as 2.3 million large limestone blocks. All of these blocks had to be cut precisely, smoothed, and then moved into position—an enormous feat of organization. As many as 25,000 to 30,000 men worked on the construction, some permanently employed by the pharaoh, with thousands more farmworkers joining them for a few months each year when the Nile flooded and they could not work their fields.

This sprawling settlement was where the thousands of pyramid builders lived during the 20 or more years it took to build Cheops' pyramid in Giza, 4,500 years ago. When completed, the pyramid stood 480.6 ft. (146.5m) high and was the tallest building in the world for more than 3,000 years.

Granary stores grain used by bakers to make the thousands of loaves of bread needed every day.

STEPS

The first pyramids in Egypt were built in a series of steps. In later reigns, the pharaohs added smooth sides, possibly to depict the rays of the Sun. The Great Pyramid was built with amazing geometrical accuracy, with its four sides lined up with true north, south, east, and west.

1. As each block was placed, the Great Pyramid rose in steps, in a style similar to the first pyramid, known as the Step Pyramid.

2. The pyramid was covered in a smooth, white limestone casing.

A cross-section reveals the complex of passages and chambers. Cheops was probably buried in the upper chamber. The chamber deep in the bedrock may have been built to mislead tomb robbers.

King's chamber

False chamber

Houses are made from mud and straw bricks and have flat roofs. The roof is also part of the home's living space.

A physician's house. Archaeologists have found evidence of broken bones that had been treated and healed.

RAMPS

The ancient Egyptians did not possess cranes or rope block and tackles, so they probably lifted the large stone blocks into place by dragging them up large ramps and then shifting them into place using levers made of wood or bronze.

Row of workers fitting stone blocks into the pyramid face.

137

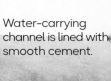
Water-carrying channel is lined with smooth cement.

ROMAN ROADS

Roman roads were built as straight as possible to provide the shortest route between locations—vital for their marching legions. Roads consisted of a number of layers and had a camber—a curved surface higher in the middle than at the edges—to drain off rainwater.

1. After a surveyor had marked the ground, a trench was dug and lined with large stones and then smaller stones.

2. A layer of concrete was then packed firmly into place by hand. The top layer was made of close-fitting paving slabs.

Wooden framework helps support a newly built arch while construction is underway.

HOW DID THE ROMANS BUILD?

The Romans were resourceful engineers. They built great networks of roads and many bridges, the largest of which, the Trajan Bridge, spanned the Danube River and was more than 0.6 mi. (1km) long.

Roman engineers planned major building works carefully before the teams of workers began baking bricks, quarrying stone, cutting wood, and mixing cement. The Romans were great innovators and developed strong concrete made from pozzolana (volcanic ash), lime mortar, and gravel. This was used in many of their structures, including about 49,700 mi. (80,000km) of roads throughout the Roman Empire. They also adopted innovations from other peoples, such as the arch, first developed by the Etruscans (an early Italian civilization), which the Romans used in bridges, aqueducts, and tunnels.

An aqueduct is built to convey constant supply clean water fro higher ground t Roman settleme The Romans use basic machines such as the leve and pulley, as w as cranes, to bu their structures.

Stones already cut to fit the arch are lowered using a polyspastos treadwheel crane.

POLYSPASTOS CRANE

The Romans built a range of different cranes to lift and lower building materials. This polyspastos crane featured a large treadwheel instead of a hand-turned winch. As a result, it could lift greater weights of up to 13,200 lb. (6,000kg).

1. Two or four men climbed into the large treadwheel and began to turn it by walking and pushing.

2. As the large wheel turned, it pulled ropes that lifted the crane's arm—and its load—upward.

ROMAN AQUEDUCT

The aqueduct could transport as much as 53 million gal. (200 million L) of water per day.

The Pont du Gard is part of a 30-mi. (50-km) -long Roman aqueduct, a structure built to transport water to the Roman settlement in Nîmes, France. Constructed of three layers of stone arches, it stands 160 ft. (49m) high and is 900 ft. (275m) long.

HOW DID ROMANS LIVE IN TOWNS?

The Romans built new towns throughout their empire, a large number of which had a similar layout. Most featured a grid of streets interconnecting at right angles with public facilities such as markets, temples, baths, and bakeries.

A shipment of slaves is offered for sale by auction.

Wealthy Romans lived in private houses, but most townspeople lived in single- or two-roomed *cenacula*. These were small apartments inside apartment blocks that were often built close together on narrow streets. Running water was rare, so most Romans used public lavatories, collected water from public fountains, and visited Roman baths. At the center of a Roman town was a large square known as a forum. This was where the government offices and law courts were situated, but it was also a place for people to meet, do business, and shop.

A residential area in a large Roman town had its own small markets and meeting places away from the central forum. Poorer Romans lived in small apartments in insulae buildings, many of which were made of wood and posed a fire risk.

PRIVATE HOME

A wealthy Roman's townhouse had a windowless outer wall and a large *atrium* (living room) with a hole in its sloping roof. This fed rainwater into a pool for drinking and washing.

Rooms looked onto an inner courtyard with a garden.

The *triclinium* was the dining room, with low couches to lie on and a place to eat.

Kitchen called a *culina*, where slaves prepared food.

Open-air hot food stalls sell meals to the many town dwellers whose homes do not have kitchens.

Craftsmen and farmers sell their goods at a local market.

HYPOCAUST

Some homes of the rich and noble, both in the city and in country villas, benefitted from a central heating system called a hypocaust, which channeled warm air around the rooms.

A furnace generated heat that traveled through a basement created by raising the floor on a series of columns called piers.

Piers made of bricks or concrete.

An important Roman travels through the town in a "litter" carried by slaves.

HOW WERE CASTLES BESIEGED?

Siege! An invading army is on the march. People have fled to the one local stronghold, an imposing stone castle. Within its stout walls may be stores of food and water, but can those inside hold out against a fierce army outside?

Many armies aimed not to destroy a castle but to capture it. Some would set up camp and secure nearby farms to feed their troops while stopping food from going in and messages from coming out. Eventually, the starving occupants would surrender. Other forces would try to tunnel under a castle's walls or use deception to gain entry. To try to shorten a long siege, archers fired volleys of arrows, some lit with burning tar, into a castle. Siege weapons, such as the trebuchet and the mangonel, rained down missiles. Often, a siege ended with a bloody storming of the castle gates and walls to get inside.

Chateau Gaillard (below) was built in northern France by English King Richard I to withstand any attack. But in 1203 to 1204, the French armies of Phillip II laid siege to the castle, battered its walls, and stormed it. The siege lasted for eight months.

Siege tower, or belfry

SIEGE TOWER

This wheeled tower was rolled up to a castle's walls. A mini drawbridge was lowered onto the ramparts. Attackers then tried to cross the bridge into the castle.

Wood or animal-hide armor, sometimes coated in mud or soaked in vinegar to resist fire

Spring-loaded mangonel catapult hurls flaming missiles and rocks.

TREBUCHET

This ingenious, catapult-like machine could hurl rocks weighing as much as two men in an arc up and over castle walls.

1. Early trebuchets were powered by people, but later models used a huge rock as a counterweight. When dropped, the weight flung a long arm upward. At the end of the arm was the weapon load, often held in a sling.

2. As the arm came over, the sling hurled the weapon at its target. Sometimes, trebuchets were loaded with dead, rotting animals to spread disease.

Weapon load flies away with great force.

Counterweight

Sling

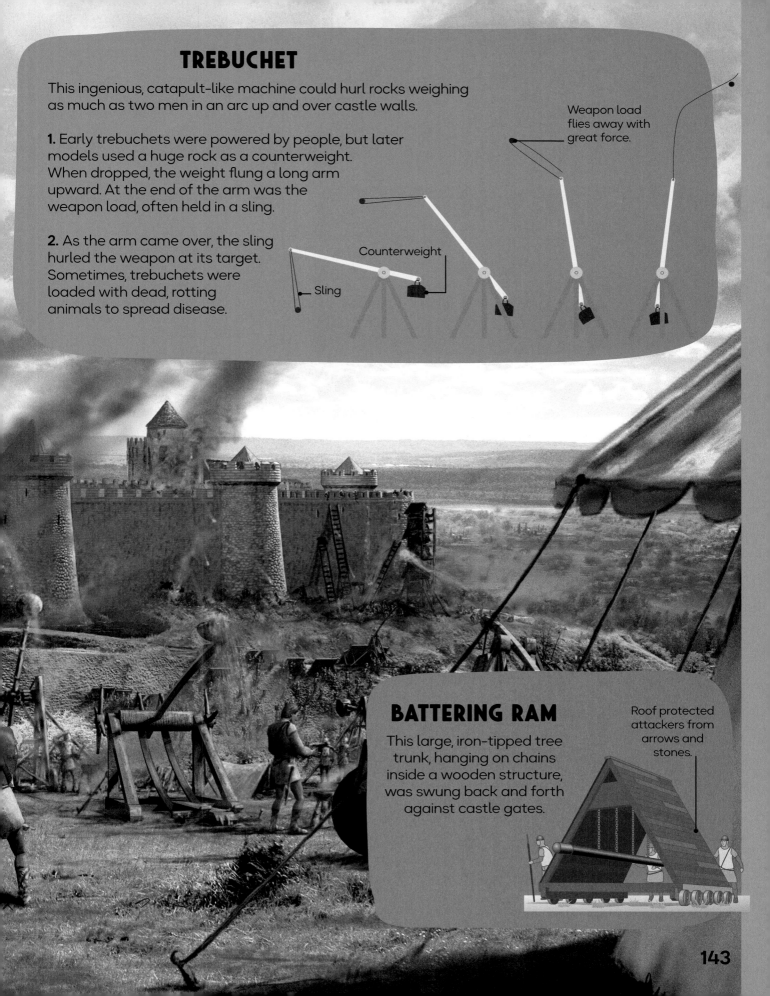

BATTERING RAM

This large, iron-tipped tree trunk, hanging on chains inside a wooden structure, was swung back and forth against castle gates.

Roof protected attackers from arrows and stones.

HOW DID THE BLACK DEATH SPREAD?

The Black Death was a devastating epidemic of the bubonic plague virus that swept through Europe and the Middle East during the 1300s. It caused the deaths of many millions of people.

A plague doctor carries a lantern and wears heavy robes and a beaked mask. The cone of the mask was filled with straw, herbs, and scents, which were thought to ward off the plague.

Bubonic plague is a disease caused by the *Yersinia pestis* bacteria, which are mostly carried by infected fleas. The fleas infest the bodies of rats, and as the rats die from the disease, the fleas, searching for food, infect humans. An outbreak of the plague may have occurred in China in the 1340s and spread to the Mediterranean, carried overseas by ships and over land by traders along common trade routes. The disease spread quickly, helped by the fact that no one knew how to treat or cure it, and by the unclean living conditions of medieval towns, where food and toilet waste was often thrown onto the streets.

People bring out their dead at night from the homes of a plague-ridden town. The populations of some cities, such as Paris and Hamburg, were halved by the Black Death, while those living in many small towns and villages were wiped out completely.

RAPID SPREAD

These maps show how quickly the disease spread throughout much of Europe, reaching Russia. A total population of four million people died.

1347

1348

1349

1353

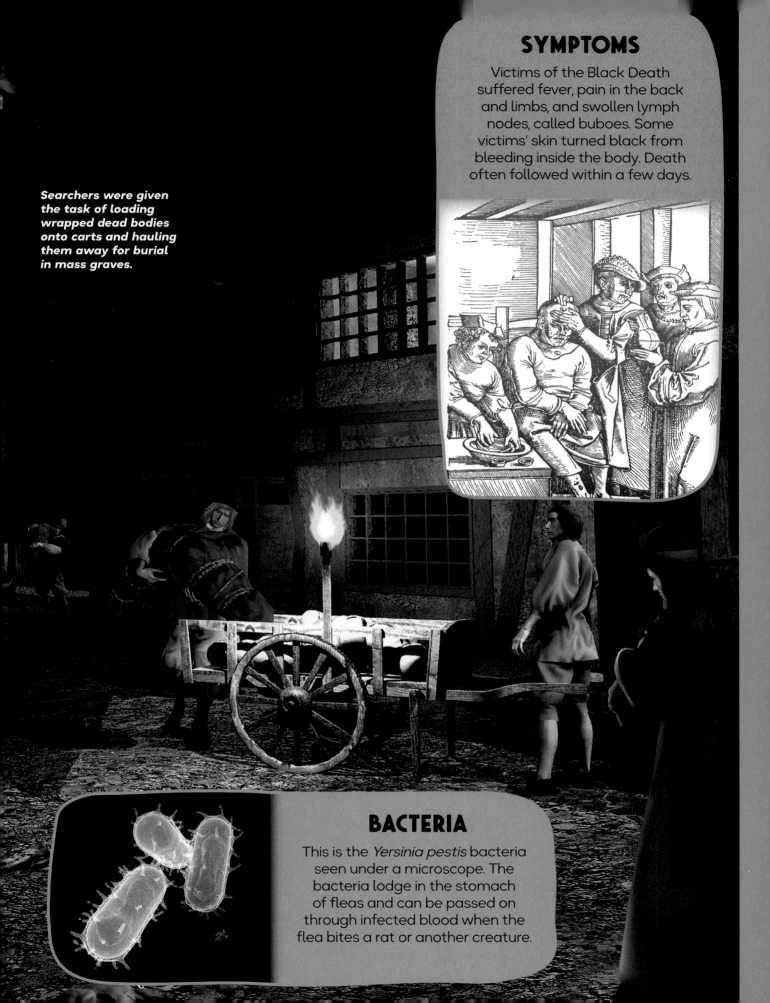

Searchers were given the task of loading wrapped dead bodies onto carts and hauling them away for burial in mass graves.

SYMPTOMS

Victims of the Black Death suffered fever, pain in the back and limbs, and swollen lymph nodes, called buboes. Some victims' skin turned black from bleeding inside the body. Death often followed within a few days.

BACTERIA

This is the *Yersinia pestis* bacteria seen under a microscope. The bacteria lodge in the stomach of fleas and can be passed on through infected blood when the flea bites a rat or another creature.

HOW DID THE INCA BUILD AN EMPIRE?

The Inca civilization emerged in the highlands of Peru in the 1200s and flourished for more than 200 years along South America's mountainous western coast. In the 1530s, its supremacy came to an end with the arrival of the Spanish conquistadors.

The Inca began expanding their territory suddenly in the 1400s under the rulers Pachacutec and, later, Túpac Yupanqui. Every male Inca had to serve in the army, and their sheer numbers overwhelmed enemies in battle. Historians also believe that the Inca used diplomacy and bargaining to extend their empire in places. The Inca were excellent engineers, using local materials to create terraced (stepped) farmlands from mountain slopes and to channel rivers for irrigation. They built about 24,850 mi. (40,000km) of trails or roads that enabled their armies and convoys of llamas carrying food and goods to travel quickly. Foot messengers were staged at posts along many roads to create a communications system.

INCA EMPIRE

At its height in the 1520s, the Inca Empire stretched from present-day Ecuador, south through Bolivia and Peru, and into central Chile and the borders of Argentina. It covered an area of 772,000 sq. mi. (2 million sq. km).

Atlantic Ocean

South America

Machu Picchu

Cusco, capital of the empire

Pacific Ocean

Granite blocks are quarried from 12 mi. (20km) away; the heaviest weigh 110 tons.

ROPE BRIDGE

This suspension rope bridge allowed the Incas to cross the deep gorge cut by the Apurímac River in Peru. The Inca were skilled at making ropes out of twisted, woven plant fibers and built rope bridges as part of their road system.

Local Inca villagers had to keep bridges in good repair as part of their service to the empire.

146

FARMING

In steep mountain regions, the Inca cut steps into the slopes and built walls to form level terraces. On these they planted crops such as sweet potatoes and maize. They also channeled mountain streams to help water these narrow farm fields.

—————— Soil shored up by stone walls

Construction of the giant Inca fortress of Sacsayhuamán was almost complete by the 1400s. This enormous stone fortress built on the edge of the Inca capital in Cusco, in present-day Peru, features walls up to 1,300 ft. (400m) long made of giant, dry rocks.

Each stone is cut carefully using hand chisels so that it fits into the wall without the need for cement or mortar. ———

The Inca have not invented the wheel, so stones are dragged using stout ropes pulled by many people.

147

BOARDING

Here, pirates use a small boat to board a merchant ship. Hooked grappling irons tied to ropes are thrown and snag onto the ship's rail, allowing the pirates to climb on board and fight to take control.

Pirates were often armed with short, curved swords—good for close fighting.

Fierce hand-to-hand fighting breaks out on deck.

Pirates climb ropes up onto ship's deck.

HOW DID PIRATES CAPTURE TREASURE?

Piracy means attacking and robbing ships at sea. It has a long history, but the 1500s to 1700s was the golden age of piracy. This was a time when galleons laden with gold crossed the Caribbean Sea and celebrated pirates sought to rob them.

Merchant ships often carried valuable cargoes of gold, silver, and spices. Pirates in the golden age would cruise the shipping routes or lurk in quiet bays, waiting to ambush such ships for their treasure or even to capture the ship for themselves. Sometimes, a pirate might use his notoriety, sailing very close and hoisting his flag to intimidate the other ship. Pirates might also fire cannon shots over the ship to force its surrender. On other occasions, they would bring their own ship alongside or use small boats to board and take over the ship and capture its valuable cargo.

Main sail catches wind to propel the 100-ft. (30-m) -long ship at high speed across the sea.

Blackbeard's flag showed a devil spearing a heart dripping blood.

Heavy cannon takes four men to operate and fires shot, each weighing 22 lb. (10kg).

Queen Anne's Revenge **was the flagship of notorious 18th-century pirate Edward Teach, known as Blackbeard. The ship had been captured by another pirate who gave it to Teach. He used it to attack and plunder more than a dozen ships in the Caribbean region and off the east coast of North America.**

CANNON

Cannon were the most powerful weapons on a ship. They used a charge of explosive, usually gunpowder, to fire a large, heavy ball—known as a shot—with great force. A 22-lb. (10-kg) shot fired from a range of 295 ft. (90m) could crash through timber 3 ft. (1m) thick.

Gunpowder

Wadding

Muzzle

Ball

Blackbeard's own living quarters are at the front (bow) of the ship and are easier to defend if attacked.

Deep hull offers plenty of storage room for food, water, captured goods, and treasure.

HOW DID CAPTAIN COOK REACH AUSTRALIA?

In 1768, Captain James Cook and 93 crew members sailed from Plymouth, England, on a three-year-long, around-the-world voyage of discovery on board the *Endeavour*.

Cook's orders were to sail to Tahiti, from where he was to search for a mysterious southern continent in the Pacific Ocean. A number of mariners had spotted parts of Australia or New Zealand, but Cook was the first to reach both and accurately chart parts of their coastlines. He was an accomplished sailor and navigator who prepared for the journey carefully, equipped with a tough ship suitable for exploration. He also took care of his crew. Many sailors of the time suffered from scurvy and other diseases caused by unclean living conditions and a lack of fresh foods. Cook insisted that his crew keep as clean as possible and eat fresh food whenever they could to ward off disease.

COOK'S ROUTE

Cook's first voyage took him across the Atlantic, around Cape Horn, and into the Pacific Ocean to Tahiti. From there, he set off to explore New Zealand and Australia. Cook stopped in Indonesia for repairs and returned home in 1771.

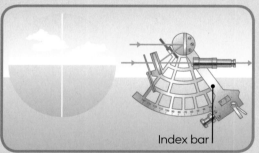

Index bar

1. Sextant is pointed toward the horizon (where sea and sky appear to meet). A swinging post—the index bar—can be moved along a curving scale marked with angles.

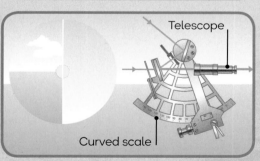

Telescope

Curved scale

2. As the index bar is moved, the image through the telescope splits in two and the Sun is brought down to the horizon. The angle can be read off the curved scale and converted into the altitude of the Sun above the horizon.

HMS Endeavour *is a former coal-carrying ship converted for the expedition. This 105-ft. (32-m) -long vessel is sturdily built and loaded with provisions and medical supplies for the long journey.*

More than 29,000 sq. ft. (2,700 sq. m) of sails allowed the ship to catch winds and travel fast.

SEXTANT AND NAVIGATION

Captain Cook used an instrument called a sextant to calculate the angle of the Sun or stars above the horizon. The angle was used with tables of star positions to calculate the ship's position.

Cook landed at Botany Bay, New South Wales, Australia, in 1770. He promptly claimed the land for the British crown.

LANDFALL

In 1769, Cook landed in New Zealand and met resistance from the native Maori, whom he decided to fight against. From there, he sailed west to Australia, landing at Botany Bay, named after the large number of new plants found there.

Hull is surrounded with a double layer of planking to protect the vessel against rocks and wood-eating worms.

Stored provisions include 10,000 cuts of beef and pork, bread, and barrels of pickled cabbage.

Broad, flat bottom allows the ship to sail well in shallow waters and to land on shores for repairs.

ENGINEERING

Other innovations of the Industrial Revolution included the use of blast furnaces to increase iron production for engines and railroads. In 1779, the first cast-iron arch bridge was built—the Iron Bridge, over the Severn River in England.

Gases from coal burning in factories escape through tall chimneys.

Large textiles factories boomed in the northwest of England in the late 1700s and 1800s. Many thousands of people moved from the countryside to towns to work in these factories.

Workers' cottages built in streets close to the factory.

RAILROADS

Steam-powered locomotives were first used to haul coal during the Industrial Revolution. From 1830, the *Rocket*, invented by Robert Stephenson, was one of the first locomotives to haul passengers on services between the cities of Liverpool and Manchester.

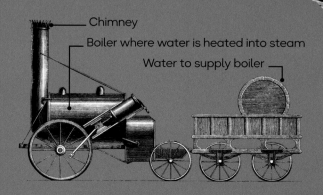

Chimney

Boiler where water is heated into steam

Water to supply boiler

Barges traveling along canals carry goods away from factories.

HOW DID STEAM POWER THE INDUSTRIAL REVOLUTION?

the Industrial Revolution began in Great Britain in the 1700s and soon spread to Western Europe and the United States. It saw the growth of large factories, which produced vast quantities of materials or goods using steam-powered machines.

The first steam engines were developed by English inventors—Thomas Savery in 1698 and Thomas Newcomen in 1712. At first, steam engines were put to work pumping water out of mines. It took the genius of Scottish inventor James Watt, and others in the 1760s onward, to create sophisticated steam engines capable of powering machines in factories. Later, larger steam engines powered the ships and trains transporting goods and materials to and from the factories.

Mill contains many floors of weaving machines powered by steam engines.

Railroads link industrial centers and big towns and cities, carrying people and materials over land.

STEAM ENGINE

In factories, steam engines were used to power giant flywheels. Belts turned by the flywheel would transfer power to the many spinning machines in a textiles mill, for example.

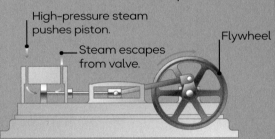

High-pressure steam pushes piston.

Steam escapes from valve.

Flywheel

1. Coal is used as fuel, which is burned in the furnace. The furnace heats the water in the tubes around the boiler.

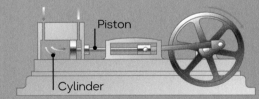

Piston

Cylinder

2. The water turns to steam that, under pressure, enters a cylinder in which it pushes a rod called a piston.

Crankshaft

3. The back-and-forth movement of the piston is turned into a turning motion by a crankshaft.

HISTORY
FIND OUT MORE ABOUT HOW THE WORLD WORKS

WEBSITES TO VISIT

www.ancientegypt.co.uk/menu.html
Check out the lives of the ancient Egyptians at these web pages hosted by the famous British Museum in London, U.K.

www.eyelid.co.uk/hiromenu.htm
Find out how to write your name using hieroglyphs and more at these web pages dedicated to ancient Egypt.

www.historyforkids.net/ancient-rome.html
Learn how the Romans lived, how their empire expanded, and much more on this large, detailed website.

http://science.howstuffworks.com/engineering/structural/10-roman-engineering-tricks.htm
Find out about construction techniques that the ancient Romans used or developed and that we still use today.

www.castles-of-britain.com/castlelearningcenter.htm
A fascinating, in-depth guide to building, defending, and living in castles, focused on the castles of Great Britain.

www.bbc.co.uk/history/british/middle_ages/black_01.shtml
Read accounts of what it was like to face the plague as it spread through the British Isles.

www.rmg.co.uk/stories/topics/what-do-pirates-do
Listen to podcasts about pirates and read up on pirate myths and facts at the U.K.'s National Maritime Museum web site.

www.boatsafe.com/history-navigation/
Follow the history of navigation at sea using this helpful website.

www.natgeokids.com/uk/discover/history/general-history/captain-cook/
Discover more about the voyages of Captain James Cook, the missions he went on, and why he is famous.

www.animatedengines.com/
Watch animations of different types of steam engines in action and read more about how the different parts work together.

INDEX

gills 76, 77, 85
glaciation 17
gravity 8, 29, 30
Great Barrier Reef 22–23

H

habitats 88, 89
hadrosaurs 48, 58, 59
hail 18, 19
hearing 56, 84
heart 90, 92
heat 26, 27
helium 26
herds 72–73, 80, 81
hieroglyphs 134, 135
high-speed train 114–115
Himalayas 16, 17
houses 108–109, 130, 137, 140–141
humans 68, 88, 90, 92–93
hunting 52–55, 82, 86, 88
hurricane 20–21
hydrogen 26, 28, 30
hypocaust 141

I

ichthyosaurs 40
Iguanodon 44, 48, 49, 51
igneous rock 9, 14
Inca 146–147

Industrial Revolution 152–153
insects 62, 69, 83
insulation 108, 109
International Space Station 122–123
ion thruster 121
iron 8, 11, 152

J

jaguars 88
jet engine 118–119
joints 92
Jurassic period 35

L

lagoon 23
lateral line 85
lava 9, 14, 15, 17
lens 95
light 26, 124
light bulbs 109
lodge 70–71
lungs 76, 90

M

Maglev train 115
magma 14, 15, 17
Maiasaurus 60–61

mammals 24, 62, 63
    marine 76
    reproduction 68–69
manta ray 76
mantle 8, 10, 11
marine animals 23, 40–41
    breathing 76–77
Mars 124, 125, 126
medical nanobot 102
meerkats 72
meteorite 9, 62
microgear 103
mid-oceanic ridge 10
migration 80–81
Millau Viaduct 110–111
Mohenjo-Daro 131
Moon 9, 126–127
motion capture 99
mountains 10, 16–17, 25
movement 44–45, 50
    speed 78–79, 92–93
mummies 132–133
muscles 44, 78, 79, 92, 93

N

nanotechnology 102–103
navigation 150
nebulae 28, 29
nervous system 94
nests 60, 61

ACKNOWLEDGMENTS

The Publisher would like to thank the following for permission to reproduce their material. Every care has been taken to trace copyright holders. However, if there have been unintentional omissions or failure to trace copyright holders, we apologize and will, if informed, endeavor to make corrections in any future edition.

Top = t; Bottom = b; Center = c; Left = l; Right = r

Cover T-rex Shutterstock/Valentyna Chukhlyebova, leaves Shutterstock/Dewin Indew, tiger Shutterstock/Setta Sornnoi, butterfly Protasov AN, pyramid iStock/WitR, waves Shutterstock/LedyX, plant iStock/Venus Kaewyoo, helicopter Shutterstock/mezzotint, parrot Shutterstock/Eric Isselee, ship Shutterstock/e71lena, big bang Shutterstock/ Four Oaks and pages 8 Shutterstock/Gerry Bishop; 12–13 Shutterstock/Fly_and_Dive; 14 Shutterstock/Claudio Rossol; 17 Shutterstock/Terry W Ryder; 21 Shutterstock/Simeonn; 22 Shutterstock/John A Anderson; 23 Shutterstock/Ethan Daniels; 25tl Shutterstock/ Chantal de Bruijne; 25tc Shutterstock/Chantal de Bruijne; 25tr Shutterstock/Israel Hervas Bengochea; 27 Shutterstock/Danshutter; 38 Dean Steadman/Kingfisher; 39 Shutterstock/ Inga Ivanova ; 40 41 Shutterstock/Morphart Creation; 41 Shutterstock/Morphart Creation; 48l Shutterstock/Elenarts; 48–49 Shutterstock/Catmando; 53 Shutterstock/Marques; 54 Shutterstock/leonello calvetti; 57 Shutterstock/Suwat wongkham; 62b Shutterstock/ FJAH; 63 Shutterstock/Catmando; 79 Shutterstock/MCarter; 81 Shutterstock/Nadezhda Bolotina; 83c Shutterstock/Hayati Kayhan; 86 Shutterstock/SusanFlashman; 89 Shutterstock/John Carnemolla; 93 Shutterstock/thelefty; 99t Shutterstock/Patricia Malina; 99b Getty/Tony Parker; 100 Shutterstock/Opsorman; 101 Shutterstock/aapsky; 103l Shutterstock/any-keen; 103r Shutterstock/Karlis Dambrans; 103br Shutterstock/Tyler Boyes; 105 Shutterstock/Andrea Danti; 106 Shutterstock/Toa55; 109 Shutterstock/Ivan Smuk; 110t Shutterstock/ Shalith; 110b Shutterstock/ Matej Hudovernik; 111 Shutterstock/ Dan Breckwoldt; 112 Getty Images/Bloomberg; 113 Shutterstock/PI; 114 Shutterstock/ i4lcocl2 ; 117 Getty/Peter Arnold; 119 Shutterstock/Martijn Smeets; 120b Shutterstock/Anton Balazh; 120c Science Photo Library/SpaceX; 121 Shutterstock/Paopano; 122c Getty Images/ Universal Images Group; 122b Getty Images/Stocktrek Images; 124 Time Life Pictures/ Getty Images; 125 NASA; 126 Getty/AFP; 131 Shutterstock/suronin; 139 Shutterstock/ StevanZZ; 145t Shutterstock/Roberto Castillo; 145b Shutterstock/Michael Taylor; 146 iStock/marktucan; 147 Shutterstock/Neale Cousland; 151 Getty Images/Hulton Archive; 152tl Shutterstock/Morphart Creation; 152b Shutterstock/Morphart Creation.

Extra art supplied by Roger Stewart.